THE ORGANIZATIONAL STRUCTURES THAT CONTRIBUTE TO SUCCESSFUL ENTREPRENEURIAL BUSINESS OPERATIONS: A QUALITATIVE EXPLORATION

A Dissertation Presented in Partial Fulfillment of the
Requirements for the Degree of
Doctor of Business Administration

By

Kevin DeVault

Colorado Technical University

May 2019

Committee

Daniel Dayton, PhD, Chair

Kurt Heppard, PhD, Committee Member

Steven Munkeby, DM, Committee Member

<u>   May 7, 2019   </u>
Date Approved

© Kevin DeVault, 2019

Abstract

This exploratory study is a look at the problem in which strategies business managers need to establish an organizational structure appropriate for entrepreneurial business operations have not been identified. The population for this study was business managers, in the Tulsa, Oklahoma area that have successfully established organizational structures for entrepreneurial business operations. The research was conducted by interviewing business managers to learn from their selection of an organizational structure, and some of the strategies that they employed. Descriptive coding was used to find common themes among the participants, to attempt to extrapolate a strategy for future entrepreneurs. Three themes emerged from the study. The first theme were myths and legends, while the second theme was the misunderstanding of limited liability in a company, and the third theme were priorities for the new entrepreneur in starting their new business venture. The five priorities are to understand tax filing status, the role of the entrepreneur in the business, organize the new business, heed startup advice, and think about the future. These five priorities give the entrepreneur areas to focus on as they are starting their entrepreneurial journey.

Keywords: *Entrepreneurship, Organizational Structure, Small Business Creation*

Dedication

First and foremost, I would like to thank my exceptionally beautiful, and incredibly understanding wife, Stephanie. Without you, I would not have been able to accomplish what I have done. I love you more than anything! To my wonderful daughters, Zoe, Madison, and Lindsey, you have inspired me in ways that you can never imagine! I hope this achievement inspires you to become amazing women, who chase after their dreams, and are only limited by their imagination and desire! To my parents, Daniel & Barbara, from an early age you knew I was special and did everything to see that I could succeed and achieve what you knew I could accomplish! Finally, to the One who has always been there, and created me to be the unique and inquiring individual that I am. Without You, I would be nothing!

Acknowledgements

I would like to thank Dr. Dayton, for guiding me through the final stretch of this journey. You took my dream and made it into a reality. To Drs Heppard and Munkeby, your feedback during the committee review process helped turn a good dissertation into a great dissertation. Finally, to all the faculty, students, and support personnel at Colorado Technical University, I can not begin to thank all of you for all the feedback, inspiration, and support that each of you gave me over the past three years as I progressed along this doctoral journey.

Table of Contents

Acknowledgements iv

Table of Contents..v

List of Tables xi

List of Figures xii

Chapter One 1

    Topic Overview/Background..2

    Problem Statement 3

    Purpose Statement 4

    Research Question 4

    Proposition 5

    Conceptual Framework...5

    Assumptions/Biases 6

    Significance of the Study..7

    Delimitations...7

    Limitations 8

    Definition of Terms 8

    General Overview of the Research Design..9

    Summary of Chapter One 10

    Organization of Dissertation...10

Chapter Two	12
Previous Dissertations	14
A Few Key Articles	15
Business Entity Selection	16
Seeking Professional Advice	18
The S Corporation	19
The Rise of the LLC	21
Taxing the LLC	23
The LLC vs. the S Corporation	23
The LLC vs. the C Corporation	25
Other Entities	25
Series LLCs	26
The Limited Liability Partnership	26
The Master Limited Partnership	27
Profit for a Cause	27
Gaps in the Literature	28
Limited Liability – A Misunderstood Concept	28
The C Corporation: More Than Double Taxation	29
Conceptual Framework	30
Summary of Literature Review	33

Chapter Three 37

    Research Tradition 37

    Research Question 39

    Research Design 39

    Population and Sample 39

    Sampling Procedure 40

    Instrumentation 41

        Validity 42

        Reliability 44

        Data Collection 45

        Data Analysis 47

        Ethical Considerations 48

    Summary of Chapter Three 49

Chapter Four 51

    Participant Demographics 51

    Presentation of the Data 52

        Participant 1 52

        Participant 2 55

        Participant 3 56

        Participant 4 57

Participant 5 57

Participant 6 58

Participant 7 62

Participant 8 67

Presentation and Discussion of Findings 69

    Theme 1 – Myths and Legends 70

    Myth 1 – Double Taxation for the C Corporation 70

    Myth 2 – Organizing the Business in Another State 71

    Theme 2 – Limited Liability Misunderstood 71

    Theme 3 – Priorities of the Entrepreneur 73

    Priority 1 – Tax Filing Status 73

    Priority 2 – Role of the Entrepreneur in the Business 74

    Priority 3 – Organizing the New Business 76

    Priority 4 – Startup Advice 76

    Priority 5 – Thinking About the Future 77

Summary of Chapter Four 79

Chapter Five 80

Findings and Conclusions 80

    Theme 1 – Myths and Legends 81

    Theme 2 – Limited Liability Misunderstood 82

    Theme 3 – Priorities of the Entrepreneur 82

        Priority 1 – Tax Filing Status 83

        Priority 2 – Role of the Entrepreneur in the Business 83

        Priority 3 – Organizing the New Business 83

        Priority 4 – Startup Advice 84

        Priority 5 – Thinking About the Future 84

Limitations of the Study 85

Implications for Practice 86

    Area 1 – Business Education for Non-Business Backgrounds 86

    Area 2 – Business Entity Research 87

Implications of Study and Recommendations for Future Research 89

    Opportunity 1 – Seeking Professional Advice 89

    Opportunity 2 – A Longitudinal Study 90

    Opportunity 3 – Seeking Experienced Business Operators 90

Reflections 91

Conclusion 91

References 95

APPENDIX A 102

    Informed Consent 102

APPENDIX B 104

Interview Questions 104

APPENDIX C 105

Interview Protocol 105

List of Tables

Table 1 *Participant Demographics*..48

Table 2 *Sources of Research*...89

List of Figures

Figure 1. Conceptual framework 31

Figure 2. Key Findings………... 92

CHAPTER ONE

The strategies entrepreneurs need to establish an organizational structure appropriate for entrepreneurial business operations have become increasingly important in business administration, especially for managers (Winrow, 2008). These skills have a vital effect in properly organizing a new business venture (Winrow, 2008). Thus, entrepreneurial business administration managers have many important responsibilities, including establishing a new business entity and determining a business organizational structure for their proposed organization (Baik, Lee, & Lee, 2015; Gesiko, 2008).

The goal of this study was to explore the strategies entrepreneurs need to establish an organizational structure appropriate for entrepreneurial business operations, from the standpoint of entrepreneurial organizations, which legal organizational structure characteristics managers consider valuable with respect to establishing a legal organizational structure (Opiela, 2004). However, legal organizational structures are often complicated by the dissimilar perceptions concerning variations in the legal organizational structures (Khandekar & Young, 1985).

The primary concern that an entrepreneurial business administration manager must resolve regarding establishing a new business venture is to ensure the business administrator selects the proper legal organizational structure (Estabrook, 2009). Thus, entrepreneurial business administration managers must have the strategies to accomplish selecting a legal organizational structure that is essential to the organization's success. Delineating the legal organizational structure needed in an entrepreneurial company is a complicated, vague, and complex issue due to the variations and nuances involved (Hansmann, Kraakman, & Squire, 2007).

The entrepreneurial organization needs a proper legal organizational structure to maintain a successful competitive edge (Johnson, 2015). However, focused research on selecting the proper legal organizational structure is needed to ensure that entrepreneurial success can be achieved (Hopson & Hopson, 2014). Without a proper legal organizational structure, the organization cannot achieve its highest calling.

Chapter 1 will formally introduce the topic of business entities as well as the main topics of this research. The problem that will need to be addressed by the research and the purpose of this study, the research question, propositions, conceptual framework, assumptions and biases, delimitations, limitations, and a few key definitions will all be addressed in Chapter 1.

Topic Overview/Background

In 2015, there were approximately 680,000 new business startups, creating 3 million new jobs (Statistics, 2018). Selecting the wrong business entity for an entrepreneur's situation could cause the business to fail, instead of succeeding (Baik et al., 2015). Many of the issues are misconceptions that are rampant in the literature and widely considered to be the truth (Johnson, 2015). By clearing up some of the misconceptions about business entities, which are prevalent in the literature, entrepreneurs, and their advisors can have a better understanding of the selection process, and what the needs of the entrepreneur are (Blair & Marcum, 2015).

Each year, hundreds of thousands of individuals decide to become an entrepreneur and go into business for themselves (Statistics, 2018). While the volume of information, as well as the access to it, on the entrepreneurship and selecting an organizational structure have improved, the success of new business ventures has not achieved the same level of expectations (Nithman, 2015). Toward this end, research investigations have indicated a gap in the knowledge that is needed to successfully establish an entrepreneurial business organizational structure (Winrow,

2008). This lack of strategy to navigate the organizational structures is creating undue hardship, which must be improved to allow entrepreneurs to be successful. Therefore, additional research is needed to create the strategies business administrators need to establish an entrepreneurial business organizational structure (Khandekar & Young, 1985).

Business administration managers have typically understood entrepreneurship. Overall, selecting an organizational structure plays a significant role that is central to entrepreneurship (Gesiko, 2008). Earlier research has exposed some strategies for selecting an organizational structure (Langemeier, 1987). Based on these findings, studies have surveyed partial strategies for selecting an organizational structure (Eyal-Cohen, 2009; Guenther, 1990).

Designing some strategies business administrators need to establish an entrepreneurial business organizational structure are an essential, critical factor to entrepreneurship's present and future survival (Estabrook, 2009). However, the differences between the various business entities continue to advance and evolve. As such, strategies and ideas need to evolve to maintain and improve current strategies business administrators need to establish an entrepreneurial business organizational structure and become more effective to entrepreneurs and business administrators (Hansmann et al., 2007).

Problem Statement

The problem that was addressed in the study is the strategies business managers need to establish an organizational structure appropriate for entrepreneurial business operations have not been identified (Winrow, 2008).

When researching a business entity, many entrepreneurs will look to the internet, but that can only give a partial picture, as the information is generic in nature, not reviewed for accuracy, and is not customizable to the needs of the entrepreneur (Opiela, 2004). Many entrepreneurs will seek professional assistance in the form of a lawyer or accountant, which can provide the customized experience to meet the needs of the entrepreneur, but there is a perception that the cost outweighs the benefits for most situations (Treusch, 2003). Further research is needed to discover the best strategies for the entrepreneur, whether that includes working with professionals to design a better pricing structure or recommending a new small business advisor that could seek to fill the void between generic books and the internet, and the perceived cost of current professional advisors.

Purpose Statement

The purpose of the qualitative exploratory study was to explore the strategies business managers need to establish an organizational structure appropriate for entrepreneurial business operations. The organizational structure is what is wrapped around the new business venture and determines how the business interacts with its environment (Hopson & Hopson, 2014). Many entrepreneurs have a sole focus on one aspect of their organizational structure, such as taxes, but are ignoring other aspects, which could be detrimental to their success. Establishing the correct legal organizational structure is paramount in the success of the new business venture (Baik et al., 2015).

Business administrators were interviewed to explore their experiences and gain a better understanding of how they establish a legal organizational structure. This exploratory study specifically looked at eight participants in Tulsa County, Oklahoma to learn from their shared experiences in establishing a legal organizational structure.

Research Question

The research question for this research was … What are the strategies business managers need to establish an organizational structure appropriate for entrepreneurial business operations?

Proposition

When an entrepreneur is researching a business entity for their new venture, there are many sources that can be used, such as the internet, books, and professional advisors (Estabrook, 2009). No one source is perfect, and each has their biases and perceptions. Even a professional advisor is going to have biases, as the professionals are looking through their own perspective (Blair & Marcum, 2015). There does not seem to be a strategy for the entrepreneur to select the best organizational structure for their needs. For this research, the proposition is that entrepreneurs need a better way of sifting through the information on the various entities, and to be able to select the best entity for their needs.

Conceptual Framework

Before the entrepreneurs begin the process of starting a new business venture, the entrepreneurs need to have an idea on what the needs for in their new business entity, in terms of ownership structure, taxes, and liability, among others (Estabrook, 2009). The entrepreneur will need to work on some issues in order to find the best entity for their situation (Hertz, Beasley, & White, 2009). Among these issues is the best organizational structure for the new business venture.

While there is a lot of research out there for the entrepreneur, the question becomes, how will the entrepreneur filters through the information and misconceptions to find a relevant organizational structure? (Johnson, 2015). Where are entrepreneurs even going to look for information in the first place (Estabrook, 2009)? There are many websites where one can go, fill out a form, pay a fee, and the website will file the paperwork to the state, while a great option for the entrepreneur who understands what the process is, the advice these sites provide is questionable at best, and many times it simply steers the entrepreneur to more products that the entrepreneur can purchase, but is that what is best for the entrepreneur or the website operator?

Past research has attempted to perform an analysis to answer these questions (Langemeier, 1987). Other research has focused on aspects, such as taxes for the small business (Eyal-Cohen, 2009). This research will focus on the strategies that the entrepreneur will need to establish their new organizational structure.

Assumptions/Biases

An assumption, in research, is a statement that is believed to be true, but is not tested (Creswell, 1998). There are three assumptions that were made for this study. The first was that a qualitative approach with an exploratory approach was an appropriate approach studying this research question. A second assumption was that the participants answered all of the questions honestly and fully understood the topic. A third assumption is that business administrators are truly interested in sharing their experiences, as a way of improving their field.

A bias is a belief that the researcher has, usually from personal experience in the field prior to the commencement of the study (Hennink, Hutter, & Bailey, 2011). The researcher has studied this field for many years and has many personal feelings on the matter. The researcher feels that much attention has been focused on certain entities, whether or not they are the best fit for the entrepreneur, and their situation. This phenomenon is what lead to the interest in this research study. In order for any biases to not influence this research, the questions needed to be written in a way to show no preference for or against a particular entity, or to be leading in nature.

Significance of the Study

Every entrepreneur who decides to start a business will go through the process of selecting a business entity and deciding on an organizational structure, or an entity will be selected for them by default (Baik et al., 2015). While there are countless books, internet articles, and information on the subject, there has been little academic research on the topic of selecting a business entity. Most of the academic research has been focused on aspects of business entity selection, such as taxes (Estabrook, 2009). While focusing on taxes can be important, there are many other aspects that also need to be considered during this process. Entrepreneurs will be served best by focusing on the whole picture, and not on one or two aspects instead. The significance of strategizing and prioritizing these aspects of the organizational structure needs to be contemplated for the benefit of future entrepreneurs.

The researcher is hoping a few distinct groups of people would benefit from this research. The first group is the entrepreneurs (Treusch, 2003). The second group is those that advise entrepreneurs when it comes to business entity selection, as this would hopefully give them a better understanding of the process (Blair & Marcum, 2015). The third group is those that are interested in the study of business, specifically Entrepreneurship. This research can provide them with more knowledge in this field, or a foundation for future research.

Delimitations

Delimitations are limitations, or bounds, placed on the research, by the researcher in order to narrow the focus (Creswell, 1998). The delimitations in this study deal with the selection criteria for the participants. Delimitation 1 is a geographic delimitation of Tulsa County for the participants. Delimitation 2 is a delimitation on the participants for their vocation and experience. The researcher interviewed 8 business managers.

Limitations

Limitations are those areas that are beyond the control of the researcher and can represent potential weaknesses in the study (Creswell, 1998). One of the limitations of this research was the honesty of the responses of the participants. A second limitation on this study was the time available for this study. A third limitation was the reliability and validity of the questions that were asked.

Definition of Terms

Business entity: A business entity is also called a legal entity, organizational structure or legal structure. It is the legal identity in which the organization operates (Khandekar & Young, 1985). It determines how the business will interact with its environment, such as how profit and taxes are calculated, how the ownership is structured, how profits can be distributed to the ownership, and whether the organization is a sperate legal entity from the ownership.

Business manager: For the purpose of this study the terms business manager, business administrator and entrepreneur were used interchangeably, and both refer to the leader of a small business startup (Johnson, 2015).

Partnership: A partnership is also called a General Partnership. It is a form of business ownership in which there is more than one owner, and the owners have not elected to file paperwork with the state electing another form of business entity (Baik et al., 2015).

Sole proprietorship: A sole proprietorship is a form of business ownership in which there is one owner, and the owner has not elected to file paperwork with the state electing another form of business entity (Baik et al., 2015).

General Overview of the Research Design

This qualitative study utilized an exploratory approach to understand the strategies business administrators need to establish an entrepreneurial business organizational structure by prioritizing the aspects of the organizational structure. This design allowed the researcher to listen to the experiences of these administrators. Exploratory studies are ideal for interviewing participants and learning from their lived experience, as a way to see if the participants have shared similar experiences (Tomkins, 2013). By interviewing the participants, the researcher was able to see if the participants have shared experiences and use those shared experiences to identify strategies business administrators need to establish an entrepreneurial business organizational structure.

The data collection began before the interview questions were asked. Once the participants were selected, the participants were provided with an introduction to the study to see if the participants were interested in participating (Thomas, Nelson, & Silverman, 2015). This also included how the interview would be recorded, to make sure that the participants are comfortable with it. Each participant was asked the same questions, allowing time for the participants to answer the question, before adding any follow-up questions thoroughly. Once all of the questions had been asked, the participants were allowed to add any thoughts they might have on the topic, as this could be an area for future research, or the participants have something pertinent, but it never came up in a question.

Data analysis began by organizing the collected information followed by data perusal, classification, and synthesis (Shenton, 2004). The data analysis approach for exploratory analysis includes (a) compiling the data from the interviews, (b) organizing the data by interviewee, (c) coding of the data (i.e., organizing the data by recognized categories), (d) identifying themes (i.e., the label attached to each recognized category), and (e) establishing data relationships (i.e., recognizing similarities and differences in themes in order to condense or separate themed categories, as appropriate) (Thomas et al., 2015). Once this process was completed, the established themed categories are the findings of the study.

Summary of Chapter One

Chapter 1 provides an overview of the topic; the problem, purpose, and research question; a brief conversation about the research design, and the conceptual framework, on which the study was be built on. The need for this study was also justified, and it also outlined potential biases, assumptions, as well as the delimitations and the limitations of the study. Finally, Chapter 1 provided a list of some of the key terms that were used for this study.

Organization of Dissertation

Chapter 1 is an overview of the topic. The need for this study was justified and outlined the research design and conceptual framework. Chapter 1 also provided some key terms, along with the potential biases, assumptions, delimitations, and limitations of the study.

Chapter 2 is a thorough look at the literature. In particular, each of the major business entities will be introduced, as well as some of their potential benefits for the entrepreneur in their venture. Many of these entities will be compared to see how differences are handled, as well as similarities. A few of the up and coming entities will also be introduced. Chapter 2 will end with a look at the gaps in the literature and a more thorough look at the conceptual framework.

Chapter 3 will be a look at the research traditions and why a qualitative research with an exploratory design was chosen for this particular study. It will also further discuss how this study was conducted, the population for this study, and how the sample was chosen. Chapter 3 will end with a look at how the participants were selected, the validity of the study, the data collection methods, how the data will be analyzed, and the ethical considerations.

Chapter 4 will look at the demographics of the study and present the data that was collected for the study. It will end with the analysis of the data and the themes that emerged from the study.

Chapter 5 will conclude the study by looking at the findings and conclusions, along with the limitations of the study. It will also look at implications for practice and implications of study and recommendations for future research. The chapter will end with some reflections and the conclusion of the study.

CHAPTER TWO

The purpose of this study was to explore the strategies business managers need to establish an organizational structure appropriate for entrepreneurial business operations (Sumutka, 1997). Before a strategy can be developed, it is imperative to have an understanding of the various common entities or structures, some of their main features, and what each of them has to offer the entrepreneur (Baik et al., 2015). This study looked at the various common business entities, as well as a few up and coming entities.

In this chapter, the literature and past research in the field of business entities will be looked at (Estabrook, 2009). To understand the research problem, it is important first to have a clear understanding of this field. There are five primary business entities; sole proprietorship, general partnership, C corporation, S corporation, and the LLC (Geekie & McClain, 2014). The literature review will focus primarily on the latter three. The other two are the default entity if the entrepreneur starts a business and does not select an entity, by filing paperwork with the state. Aspects of the sole proprietorship and partnership will be addressed with the other three entities, as well in the general entity selection section.

For this study, the literature is derived from a variety of sources. The research looks at an overall discussion on business entity selection, including what the entrepreneurs should be looking for, and questions the entrepreneurs should be asking (Blair & Marcum, 2015). In addition, the literature also consists of articles that were primarily written about one particular entity or were a comparison of two entities, as these would provide foundational material on the various entities (Hertz et al., 2009). The majority of the source material came from peer-reviewed journals, usually written for a specific industry, such as insurance or banking.

The literature review will start with a look at some of the previous dissertations in this field, while the next section will look at a few key articles that have helped shaped this research (Hertz et al., 2009; Langemeier, 1987). After this intro to the field, the literature will be looked at for selecting a business entity, as well as some of the questions that the entrepreneur needs to be asking themselves as the entrepreneurs are going through this process (Blair & Marcum, 2015). This part will also look at some of the issues when seeking professional advice in assistance of selecting an entity, and some of the areas where a professional can help the entrepreneur.

The next part of the literature review will look at some of the specific entities, starting with the S corporation, followed by the LLC (Alberty, 2003). For both entities, the history will be looked at, as well as some of their key features that these entities offer the entrepreneur (Chrisman, 2010). After looking at each of them separately, the entities will be compared to see how the entities differ from one another in some of the key areas that would impact an entrepreneur (Banoff & Lipton, 2003). The LLC will also be compared to the C corporation in the next section, mostly in the area of taxes and how the profits can be distributed to the owners. This is important as the LLC has the option of being taxed as a C corporation, and it is important to see the difference.

The last section of the literature review will look at some of the gaps in the literature. These gaps are areas where there is not a lot of research, or there are a lot of misconceptions and where what many people believe is true is not reality. The first gap or misconception that will be looked at is the concept of limited liability (Misenti, 2016). What liability is limited, and what liability is not? The second misconception is in the C corporation (Raible, Teti, & Brinker, 2015). Even though people deal with them on a regular basis, few really understand them, and this includes many professionals who advise entrepreneurs. Some of the misconceptions of the C corporation will be looked at to show some of the features that will be beneficial to the entrepreneur, especially in the startup phase.

The concluding section of the literature review will be the conceptual framework. The conceptual framework will visualize the business entity selection process, as well as a narrative for how it should work (Estabrook, 2009). Unfortunately, it does not always work as will be seen with the gaps in the literature. There are many unanswered questions about the entity selection process that will also be looked at during the conceptual framework, in order to gain a better understanding of some of the issues in this field that needs to be addressed, and hopefully some of these questions can be addressed and possibly answered through this research (Gesiko, 2008).

Previous Dissertations

Before looking through the literature, the researcher felt it would be prudent to look at some of the previous work that others have done in this field. There have been countless research done on the various business entities, but not as much as been done when it comes to selecting a business entity (Langemeier, 1987). There seems to be a disconnect in this field between the world of academia, and the practitioners of this field, who have done much of the research in this field (Geekie & McClain, 2014).

The only other dissertation that closely matches this area of interest was done over 30 years ago, and it was a quantitative look at the business entity selection and focused on the sole proprietorship, partnership, and the S & C corporation (Langemeier, 1987). This research was qualitative in nature and focused on the LLC and the S & C corporations. Arguably the most popular entity today, the Limited Liability Company (LLC), was not even mentioned in the previous research, as only two states had enacted legislation at that time (Chrisman, 2010).

While the dissertation mentioned above was the only one that looked directly at business entity selection, there have been others that had looked at aspects of business entity selection (Guenther, 1990). This research was looking primarily at how income taxes affect one's choice of business entity. While many do consider income taxes to be a primary factor in the selection of a business entity, as seen recently with the recent tax cuts, tax rates can easily be changed with a simple majority of Congress, and as such, should not be the primary factor for deciding on a business entity, but should instead be something that is looked at along with the other factors, such as those that will be looked at later in the literature review (Estabrook, 2009).

The final dissertation that will be looked at also was looking at taxes (Eyal-Cohen, 2009). This report focused more on the S corporation, which was created as an alternative to the C corporation. The S corporation offered many of the benefits of the C corporation, but had pass-through taxation, as opposed to separate corporate tax rates, followed by taxes on dividends (distributions to the shareholders or owners of the company) (Burton & Karlinsky, 2007). This research, however, focused on more than one type of entity.

A Few Key Articles

When working on this dissertation, there were a few key articles that affected not only the research, but also affected how the researcher has approached this topic. With the researcher, there were two articles that a profound impact on the research. The first was what the researcher calls a foundation article, as it was one of those articles that even though it is dated, researchers are still using it for their research (Khandekar & Young, 1985). The other article really changed how the researcher approached this topic, and how the researcher decided to research this topic (Hertz et al., 2009).

When the researcher first started researching this topic, the researcher would read various sources, then look to see what sources the authors had used to write their article, as a way of finding more sources, and also as a way to see what articles were important in this field. When the researcher did this, one article kept repeatedly appearing, even though it was over 20 years older than the article that was being written. The researcher needed to find out why something written in 1985 was still relevant today. After examining the article (Khandekar & Young, 1985), the researcher could see why it is still relevant. Unlike many of the articles that will be covered later, this one is unbiased in its presentation of the entities and is also very analytical in how it approaches the selection of the entities, something that is often overlooked today, where many are emotionally driven (Hopson & Hopson, 2014).

Another article that has had a profound impact on the research provided much information that directed how to research the topic (Hertz et al., 2009). At the end of the article, there is a section on future research, which spells out a qualitative research, the people that need to be interviewed, as well as some of the questions that can be asked. Unlike in previous research, the researcher would not need to do a quantitative analysis but could instead do a qualitative (Langemeier, 1987).

Business Entity Selection

For many entrepreneurs, this is one of the first decisions that the entrepreneurs will make for their new business venture, but one that is often overlooked in the process of getting their company up and running (Estabrook, 2009). As mentioned in the introduction to the chapter, there are many things about the business that are determined by the type of business entity that the entrepreneur uses (Geekie & McClain, 2014). This section will examine some of the questions that the entrepreneur should be asking, as well as some of the major topics that the business entity will have an impact on.

Choosing a business entity for a newly formed business is a strategic decision, and the costs and benefits of each entity need to be considered, as well as the unique situation of the business itself (Geekie & McClain, 2014). The ownership structure is one of the more important decisions, and one that is often overlooked. On the one hand, the sole proprietor has absolute control, but unlimited liability can hamper the raising of funds (Baik et al., 2015). On the other hand, the C corporation has limited liability, easier access to capital, but its structure can make it harder to make important decisions quickly due to their level of formality, with the board of directors' approval for major decisions.

Another often-overlooked consideration in the selection of a business entity is the full life cycle of the business (Estabrook, 2009). Many entrepreneurs simply think about today, and not what the future holds, or where their new business will be in the future. The right entity for a situation is one that offers maximum liability protection while at the same time providing for the largest return on investment (Gesiko, 2008).

There are many threshold issues that need to be looked at when selecting a business entity, and include the control of ownership and management, management of risk, fringe benefits that are paid by the company, cost, and simplicity, and finally taxation (Sumutka, 1997). There is a three-fold approach to selecting an entity; (a) look at each one from an overall standpoint, and consider the pros and cons of each; (b) look at the specific income tax treatment of each at the venture level and owner level; and (c) weigh the tax advantages and disadvantages against the nontax issues, making sure all the issues are addressed (Treusch, 2003).

When it comes to the most crucial factor in selecting a business entity, at least to the entrepreneur, taxes seem to take the lead (McNulty & Kwon, 2006). The primary difference between the S corporation and the C corporation is how taxes are handled and who pays them (Hodder, McAnally, & Weaver, 2003). State and local taxes can also come into play when deciding on a business entity, as states have different tax rates, and can treat one entity more favorably when it comes to taxes (Luna & Murray, 2010). Selecting the right structure can free more money for both the owner, as well as the employees (Donohoe, Lisowsky, & Mayberry, 2015).

Besides income taxes, there are other taxes that the selection of a business entity has an impact on. Some of the entities can pay the owner a reasonable salary, and the owners can deduct the salary and associated employment taxes as an expense of the company (Altieri & Cenker, 2002). Some of the other specialty issues will be looked at during the review of each of the entities. While it is possible to convert to a different entity later on, and many do, there are many tax considerations that need to take place to ensure a smooth transition (Sellers & Tripp, 2015).

Seeking Professional Advice

While entrepreneurs are often advised to seek professional advice, the advice can be one-sided, depending on whom the entrepreneurs see. Accountants and other financial professionals tend to focus on the tax issues, whereas attorneys tend to focus on nontax issues, such as ownership structure, liability issues, and the framework that the venture will operate under (Blair & Marcum, 2015). Changes to the tax law, as well as new case law, can make the best entity for a situation a moving target (Opiela, 2004). In addition, since most of the entities are a creation of state statutes, the entities can and often change, and new entities can be created (Winrow, 2008).

Entrepreneurs that have significant assets also need to seek professional advice on how to protect their personal assets as well as understand how estate planning is impacted by their selection of a business entity (Hopson & Hopson, 2014). If the entrepreneur would like their business to become a family business that is run by future generations, then that needs to be taken into consideration when selecting an entity (Jurinski, 2004). Many entrepreneurs do not take into account their future plans when selecting an entity (Treusch, 2003).

The S Corporation

The first entity that will be looked at in detail is the S corporation, sometimes called the small business corporation (Stancil, 2012). It is one of the older entities that are available to today's entrepreneurs, and it was one of the first ones that were created with the small business owner in mind, in an attempt to give the small business owner many of the features that Congress thought would make them more successful (Evans & Castilla, 2013). Congress created the S corporation in 1958, as an alternative to the regular or C corporation (Stancil, 2012). The S corporation is created by filing paperwork with the state to incorporate, just as in the case of the C corporation, and is, in fact, a C corporation at creation, but the corporation files Form 2553 with the IRS to elect to become an S corporation (Samson & McLeod, 1990).

The S corporation is a pass-through entity, unlike the C corporation, and has a few restrictions, such as a limit of 100 shareholders, only one class of stock, and who can be a shareholder (Evans & Castilla, 2013; Schnee, 2006). Like the C corporation, the owners of the S corporation can be employed by the corporation, and receive a salary and benefits, and the amount of salary is subject to FICA taxes, but any profits paid to the shareholders are not subject to FICA taxes, which is different from the other pass-through entities (Alberty, 2003). The IRS does expect the business to pay a reasonable salary, so that FICA taxes can be collected (Fellows

& Jewell, 2007). Failure to do so can result in the IRS assigning a salary and imposing FICA taxes on the salary (Burton & Karlinsky, 2007). The IRS can also find that non-salary payments made to the owner/ employee are indeed salary payments if a reasonable salary was not paid, but instead interest payments and rent were paid to the owner as a way of avoiding FICA taxes, and will then recategorize the payments as salary, chargeback FICA taxes, as well as interest and penalties on those back taxes (Geisler & Wallace, 2005).

Unlike the C corporation, if the S corporation pays the medical insurance for the shareholder, the business can deduct the expense, but the shareholder must include the payments on their W2, but the distributions are not subject to FICA taxes (Karlinsky & Burton, 2008). Owners of 2% or more of the S corporation are not treated as employees when it comes to paying many fringe benefits, but are instead treated as partnerships, and like the owners of an LLC, and other pass-through entities, are unable to offer many of the fringe benefits that the C corporation can pay (Anderson, 2004). Unlike the other pass-through entities, the S corporation is able to offer an employee stock ownership plan (ESOP), as long as it benefits all of the employees (Shanney-Saborsky, 1998).

What makes the S corporation unique, is that the tax regulations that govern it are under a separate section of the IRS tax code (subchapter S), whereas all the other pass-through entities are governed by subchapter K of the IRS tax code (Schwidetzky, 2009). The C corporation gets its name because its tax regulations are in subchapter C of the tax code. Even though the S corporation is a pass-through entity, when it comes to non-tax regulations, it is governed by subchapter C, just like the C corporation (McMahon & Simmons, 2014). It is easier to think of an S corporation, as a regular corporation, with the major difference, is in how it is taxed.

As of 2014, almost three-quarters of the corporations were in fact S corporations (Sicular, 2014). For the past 20 years, it was the most popular entity other than sole proprietorships (Banoff & Lipton, 2003). If current trends continue, it will soon be passed by the next entity that will be looked at, the Limited Liability Company.

The Rise of the LLC

The next entity that will be looked at is the Limited Liability Company (LLC) (Riles & Whitlock, 2003). What makes it different from the S corporation is that it is a creature that was created by state legislatures, and not by Congress (Johnson, 2015). While it had a slow start, after the IRS gave it a favorable tax decision, it quickly gained acceptance in the states, and is today considered the first choice for many entrepreneurs. This section will look at the history of the LLC, some of its features, and end with a look at how it is taxed.

Wyoming is credited with the creation of the Limited Liability Company (LLC) in 1977 (Schatz, Gorski, & Schatz, 1996). The LLC was to be a hybrid entity that offered the benefits of the corporation but was treated as a partnership (Chrisman, 2010). At the end of 1990, four states had LLC legislation on the books, and by the end of 1996, it had grown to 48 states and the District of Columbia (Karl, 1999).

The LLC is like the corporations in that the LLC is created by filing paperwork with the state and paying a filing fee, though the paperwork is called an Articles of Organization, as opposed to an Articles of Incorporation for a corporation (Rothman, 2007). For some reason, the cost to file to create an LLC is on average seventeen percent higher, than the cost of filing to form a corporation (Blair, Marcum, & Fry, 2009). While it may not seem like a lot, it could sway the small business owner in their decision on which entity the entrepreneur want to use for their new business. The owners of an LLC are called members, whereas the owners of a corporation are called shareholders (Karl, 1999). The LLC, like the corporation, also offers its owners limited liability from the debts of the business as well as the negligent acts that the other members commit while acting on behalf of the business (Summa, 1996).

One of the reasons why the LLC has become as popular as it has is that it offers a lot of flexibility, which the other entities cannot offer. Unlike the corporation, there are no required board of director meetings, nor shareholder meetings (Cruz & Karayan, 1996). The LLC can either be managed by the members (owners), or the members can hire a manager (CEO) to run the LLC (Leimberg, 1994) The operating agreement, similar to a partnership agreement or corporate bylaws, will lay out how the LLC will be managed, and how other areas of the LLC will be handled, and should address issues such as how the business should operate, if there are multiple partners, the four Ds need to be addressed (Miller, 2014). The four D's are the death of a partner, disability of a partner, divorce of a partner (as their former spouse could receive a share of the business or a payout equal to a share of the business), and finally, a partner becomes disinterested in the business and wanting to leave.

The LLC has grown exponentially since states started adopting the LLC statutes in the early '90s. In 1990 about 70% of active businesses were corporations, while the remaining were partnerships (Gomtsian, 2015). Today, it is about 57% corporation, 12% partnership, and 31% LLC (Chrisman, 2010). It is difficult to calculate the number of sole proprietorships since sole proprietorships are not created by filing something with the state, and no forms are filed with the IRS other than the personal 1040 (Altieri & Cenker, 2002). Those numbers also do not include LLCs that are taxed as corporations.

Taxing the LLC

When it comes to paying Federal income taxes, the owners of the LLC have a few options. If there are two or more owners, the company can be treated like a partnership for income tax purposes, or the company can elect to be treated as a corporation for income tax purposes, either the C or even S corporation (Chrisman, 2010; Gilbert, 2008). If there is only one owner, and the company does not elect corporate income tax treatment, either C or S, the company will be considered a disregarded entity, and any income/ losses will simply pass to their personal 1040 on schedule C as business income or loss (Nevius, 2007; Ostrov, 2000). The IRS considers a single member LLC as a disregarded entity, and all of the assets, liabilities, income, and deductions belong to the individual owner (McMahonn, 2012).

The LLC vs. the S Corporation

As seen in the previous sections, there are many similarities between the LLC and the S corporation, though there are many differences (Altieri & Cenker, 2002). In this section, the differences will be the focus. The first difference that will be looked at is the way the ownership is structured, along with ownership limitations (Gesiko, 2008). This will be followed by a look at the differences in formalities that need to be observed. Differences in how the owners are paid will be the next sections, and it will end with a cautionary word regarding the age of the LLC, and some of the problems that it represents (Wells & Yoshimoto, 1993).

One of the downsides of the S corporation is the limit on the ownership, such as the number and type, which is something that the LLC does not have to deal with, in fact, S corporations, C corporations, partnerships, other LLCs, trusts and estates can all be owners of an LLC (Cleveland, Wells, & Yoshimoto, 1996). This phenomenon is something that is now being exploited to create a new type of LLC, which will be looked at later. Some of the ownership restrictions on the S corporation are that owners are limited to one hundred shareholders, only one share of stock, and only US citizens or resident aliens (Campbell, 1994).

Another benefit to the LLC is the lack of corporate formalities that are required to be met, such as annual meetings for shareholders and the board of directors, minutes from meetings, corporate resolutions for major decisions, or other records of transactions, though the LLC does need to have records of ownership, and maintain a separation from the owner's personal assets and the business' assets (Petravick & Troutman, 2007). The LLC also does not have to worry about passive income limitations in the way that the S corporation does, making it an ideal entity for placing rental real estate in (Wells, 1994). Since the LLC can be taxed as an S corporation, it is possible to have the benefits of the LLC, while gaining some of the benefits of being taxed as an S corporation (Chrisman, 2010). One such benefit is reduced self-employment taxes. The owners in an S corporation can be paid a reasonable salary, and Social Security and Medicare taxes will be paid on the salary, but not on the rest of the profit, while the owners of the LLC will pay those taxes on their entire share of the profit, but only if the owners are actively running the LLC (Riles & Whitlock, 2003).

There is one area where the LLC is at a disadvantage over the S corporation, and the other entities for that matter (Opiela, 2004). Twenty-eight years ago, the LLC was only available in four states, and it was only in the late 1990's that it became available in all fifty states (Chrisman, 2010). There are many issues that still need to be worked out as the issues come along, and either the states legislatures, tax agencies, or the courts will need to address these issues and settle them, whereas much of the case law dealing with partnerships and corporations have been settled over the decades and centuries that these entities have been available (Wells & Yoshimoto, 1993).

The LLC vs. the C Corporation

While many entrepreneurs are not considering starting with a C corporation, there are some differences between the LLC and the S corporation that are worth mentioning (Raible et al., 2015). One is the LLC can be set up to be taxed as a C corporation (Ellentuck, 2010). This next section is considered a comparison of pass-through taxation for an LLC, and corporate taxation for the LLC (Everett, Raabe, & Hennig, 2011).

The primary difference between the two is how taxes are calculated and paid, as well as how the owners receive their share of the profit. If the LLC is set up as a pass-through entity, which the majority are, then the profits are calculated at the end of the year, and the owners will pay income tax on their share of the profit, whether or not the money was actually paid to them (Ellentuck, 2010). In the C corporation, at the end of the tax year the profit is calculated and the tax paid on it, and then any distributions in the form of dividends would be taxed as income on the owner's personal income tax return, hence the dreaded double taxation, but many small businesses that are run as a C corporation will pay the owners a reasonable salary, which is deductible to the business unlike the dividend, and also reducing their corporate tax liability (Lynch, Casten, & Beausejour, 2012). In addition to the above income tax issues, the LLC owners are also responsible for paying the full Social Security and Medicare taxes on their share of the profit, also called self-employment taxes, even if no profit is paid out, which is why many LLCs will pay enough profit to the owners to cover the taxes that will need to be paid (Everett et al., 2011).

Other Entities

While the above entities are the primary ones that an entrepreneur will consider when selecting an entity, there are a few others that are worth mentioning. Most of them are a variation of the LLC (Bahena, 2010). The series LLC is multiple LLCs that are put together to form one large company, while the Limited Liability Partnership is similar, but often used by professionals such as doctors and attorneys that want to organize, but still have limited liability (Altieri & Cenker, 2002). The master limited partnership is a way for a corporation to offer an investment directly to the public for a particular project, as opposed to investing in the company as a whole (Collins & Bey, 1986). The last entity is a newer idea of allowing a for-profit company to engage in some non-profit areas and do good, without upsetting shareholders that the profit is not going to them, but instead to the greater good (Artz & Sutherland, 2010).

Series LLCs

As mentioned earlier in the discussion of the Limited Liability Company, another LLC can own an LLC (Cleveland et al., 1996). This has led to the creation of the Series LLC, which is a master LLC that owns several subsidiary LLCs (Nevius, 2010). A company that owns a lot of real estate could use the master LLC to operate the company, but the company would keep the real estate in separate subsidiary LLCs (Bahena, 2010). In theory, this could insulate much of the assets from a creditor who has a claim on one particular LLC, though with only about a third of states offering the Series LLC, and the relatively new status, the jury is still out on many of the liability and tax issues (Land, 2009).

The Limited Liability Partnership

The limited liability partnership (LLP), is very similar to the LLC, but there must be at least two partners, and in some states the partners that are active in running the business may not have the same limited liability that the owners would have in an LLC (Hansmann et al., 2007). In some states, certain professionals, such as doctors, lawyers, and accountants cannot form an LLC, but must instead form an LLP (Openshaw, 2002). One variation is the Family Limited

Partnership, wherein a family has control over some assets, and can pass down control to future generations, while attempting to save on taxes on the generational transfers, though the generational transfers have come under IRS scrutiny as of late (Jurinski, 2004).

The Master Limited Partnership

The master limited partnership is a limited partnership that is publicly traded, and the limited partners can buy shares or units (Collins & Bey, 1986). It is used almost exclusively in the energy sector, as a way to find investors that can invest directly in a project. The limited partners receive limited liability as owners, while the owners/ investors can directly receive profits from their investments, while also bypassing corporate taxes (Henzler & Milani, 2014). The general partner, usually a corporation, will have access to the capital markets to find investors for particular projects, and payments to the partners up to their original investment are not taxable.

Profit for a Cause

A new type of entity, the Low-Profit Limited Liability Company (L_3C), is blurring the lines between the for-profit company, and the non-profit company (Vaughan & Arsneault, 2018). The L_3C takes the concept of corporate social responsibility to a new level, and while the entity is generating profit, the profit is being used for social benefit causes (Artz & Sutherland, 2010). Because of their social cause, the L_3C are often able to receive funding from foundations for their causes. Socially conscious entrepreneurs see this as a way to protect themselves from the standard fiduciary responsibility to maximize profits for the shareholders (Andre, 2012). In addition to the fiduciary duty to the shareholders, the L_3Cs are now obligated to pursue public benefit (Hiller, 2013).

Gaps in the Literature

After looking through the research, the researcher felt that there were some gaps in the literature that warranted further research. The first is the concept of limited liability, which is one of the primary reasons that an entrepreneur seeks a formal structure such as the LLC for their entity (Nithman, 2016). Many entrepreneurs do not understand this concept and sadly, there is not much truthful discussion on the topic. The only liability that is limited is their personal assets, which are protected from debts the company occurs, but this falsehood of limited liability could really hurt the entrepreneur if the entrepreneur does not understand what liability is limited and which liability is not and can never be limited (Johnson, 2015).

The second gap in the literature is in the C corporation. Even though it has been around for some time, few people including professionals really understand it, and what it can offer to the entrepreneur (Lamoreaux, 1998). Everyone gets caught up in the double taxation, and leaves it at that when there is more to the C corporation than a feature, which in reality does not even impact the majority of small business entrepreneurs (Raible et al., 2015).

Limited Liability – A Misunderstood Concept

One of the primary reasons that an entrepreneur decides to seek a formal business entity is the promise of limited liability for the owners. In a sole proprietorship and a general partnership, the owner or owners can be held personally liable for the acts of the organization, and in a partnership, one partner can be held jointly and severally liable for the debts and actions of the other partners (Nithman, 2015). While this is generally the case, there are a few exceptions that many entrepreneurs are unaware of, which could cost them.

The first exception is in the case of fraud, such as a corporation that is set up to run an illegitimate business (Nithman, 2016). Another area where limited liability does not cover the owners is when the owner personally guarantees a loan or lease, which is often quite possible for a new business (Johnson, 2015). If the entrepreneur defaults on one of these loans, their personal assets can be put in jeopardy (Nithman, 2017).

The final area where limited liability does not cover the owners is in the commission of a tort (Misenti, 2016). A common example would be a florist, who is the owner of a corporation. If the owner was the driver during a delivery and caused an accident, the corporation could be sued, and the driver could be sued, not as the owner, but as the employee that caused the accident. If the court found against the owner/driver, all of their personal assets could be in jeopardy, even though the owners have limited liability through their entity. Having proper insurances can often protect an individual better than having limited liability through an entity (Nithman, 2015).

The C Corporation: More Than Double Taxation

The C corporation is one of the oldest forms of business entities, after the partnership and the sole proprietorship (Lamoreaux, 1998). Before the 1870s, corporations came about from receiving a charter from the government to operate as a corporation. In the 1870s the laws were relaxed, and companies no longer needed a charter from the government in order to form a corporation (Raible et al., 2015).

What sets the C corporation apart from the other entities is how profits are taxed. Profits are initially taxed at the entity level, using a separate set of tax rates than the personal rates that individuals pay, or pass-through entities pay (Raible et al., 2015). At profits that are distributed to the owners will then be paid, and are not deductible to the corporation, and are also taxable to the owner, thus the dreaded double taxation (Evans & Castilla, 2013). When most people discuss business entities, double taxation is mentioned, then move on to something else. This thinking is so prevalent that most advisors steer their clients away from the C corporation, simply because of this. When reviewing the literature, the vast majority of scholarly articles also preach this, and it is to the point, where the researcher feels it is a serious gap in the literature.

What many small business C corporations do to avoid the double taxation, is make the owner an employee of the company, which is the only entity that is allowed to do so (Jenkins, 1988). The owner is then paid a reasonable salary, which is a deductible expense to the corporation, unlike dividends. This method of paying the owner is called income splitting. As an example, the owner of a C corporation could have a profit before a salary of $200,000. For every other entity, the profit of $200,000 will be paid on their personal income tax. For the C corporation, the owner could be paid a salary of $100,000 throughout the year, leaving the corporation with $100,000 in profits that are taxed, and the remainder is retained for future needs. Because of the way that the C corporation is taxed, and the way that dividends are taxed, for many small corporations, it can be cheaper to pay the corporate tax and the taxes on dividends (Calcagni, 2010).

Another benefit that is only available to the C corporation that is often overlooked are many of the write-offs that the business can deduct (Raible et al., 2015). There are many benefits, such as medical insurance, that are deductible to the business, and not taxable to the owner/ employee of the C corporation, but that would be taxable to other entities (Nithman, 2016). This is another area that many potential entrepreneurs are unaware of, and would be of help to many, to be able to write-off things that the owner would need to purchase anyway.

Conceptual Framework

Figure 1 is the diagram for the process that an entrepreneur would go through when selecting a business entity. Before the entrepreneurs begin, the entrepreneurs need to have an idea of what the entrepreneurs are looking for in their new business entity (Estabrook, 2009).

The second column represents some of the issues that the entrepreneurs need to work through in order to find the best entity for their situation (Hertz et al., 2009). The third column represents some of their possible choices for their new entity, based on their needs from the second column.

The graphical framework represents the process that should happen, but as seen in the literature review, there are a few gaps that are interfering with this process. One of the gaps is the concept of limited liability (Misenti, 2016). Many, including many professionals, do not fully understand what liability is limited and what liabilities are not. The other concept is the C corporation and its unique tax structure (Raible et al., 2015). Many advisors feel that this complicated tax structure is too complex for an entrepreneur to handle, or the advisors do not fully understand the unique opportunities that the C corporation can bring to a new business venture and move on to something else. When close to half of the second row is not readily understood by the entrepreneur or their professional advisors, how can the entrepreneurs be expected to make the best decision on the choice of a business entity?

While there is much research out there for the entrepreneur, the question becomes, How will the entrepreneur filter through the bad information and misconceptions to find the relevant information? (Johnson, 2015). Where are entrepreneurs even going to look for information in the first place (Estabrook, 2009)? There are many websites where one can go, fill out a form, pay a fee, and the website will file the paperwork to the state, while a great option for the entrepreneur who understands what the process is, the advice these sites provide is questionable at best, and many times it simply steers the entrepreneur to more products that the entrepreneur can purchase, but is that what is best for the entrepreneur or the website operator?

If the entrepreneur seeks professional advice, many of the same problems are still there. As seen in the literature review, attorneys tend to focus on ownership structure, operating agreements, and other legal issues, while financial professionals tend to focus on the financial aspects, such as taxes and profit distributions (Blair & Marcum, 2015).

This gap in the literature is something that the researcher has experienced firsthand, which is why the researcher wants to research this field so that others can avoid some of the frustrations that the researcher had to experience himself. The researcher found too many websites had contradictory information, and there was much that the researcher had to learn on their own. There are many exceptional circumstances when an entrepreneur would want to have a formal entity, or when a C corporation would be ideal, but some of these issues have not been addressed at all in the literature, or even online (Raible et al., 2015).

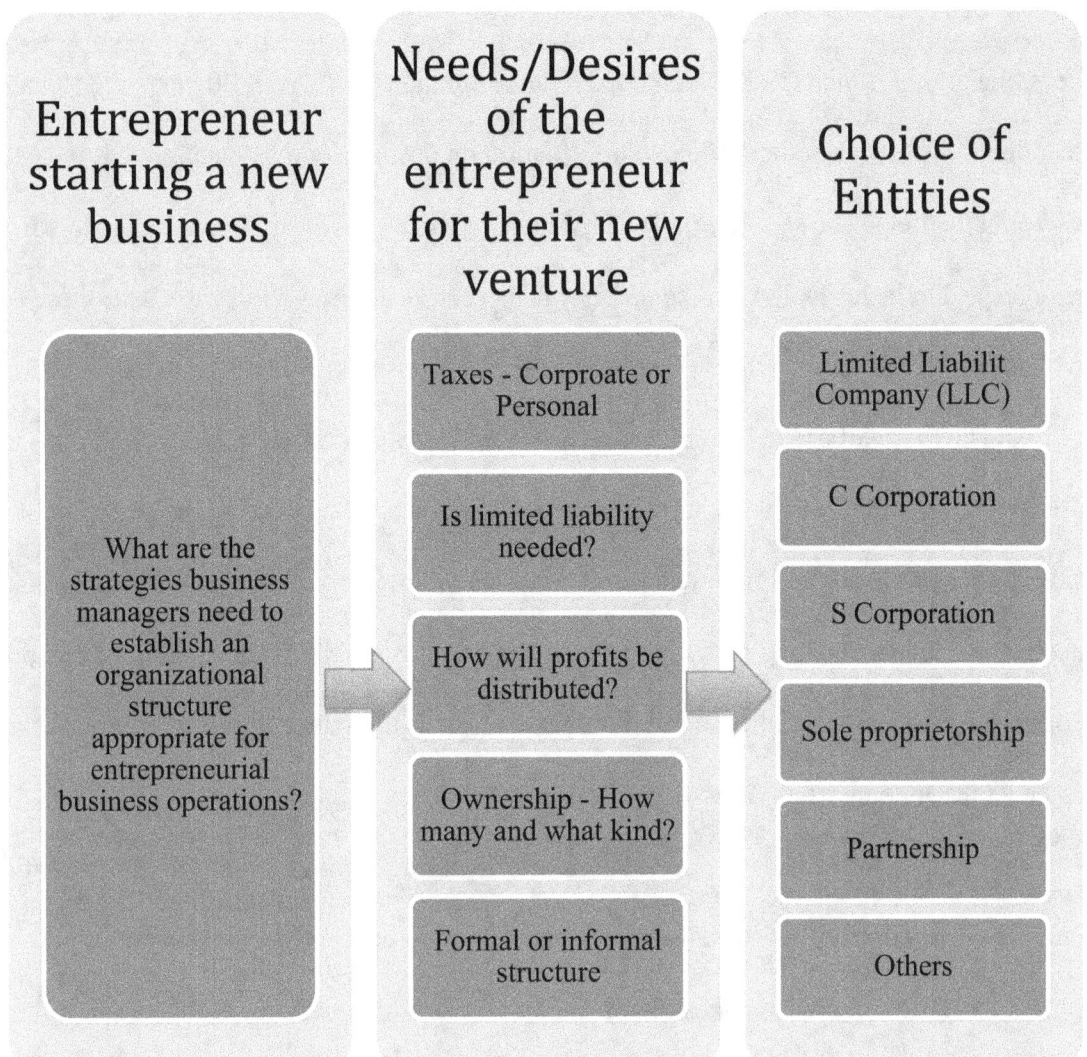

Figure 1. Conceptual framework.

Summary of Literature Review

There was a lot of information in the literature review. The literature review started with a review of some of the previous dissertations and saw that there had not been much academic research in this field, and what little bit is there, is outdated (Langemeier, 1987). There have been many dissertations that have looked at aspects of small business creation, such as taxes, and small business creation in general (Eyal-Cohen, 2009).

Before diving into the literature review, two key articles were looked. The first was a keystone article, which is still being cited today even though it is over 30 years old (Khandekar & Young, 1985). It has such valuable information on business entity selection that it is still useful in the field. The second article shaped the way that the researcher looked at this field, and it suggested to instead talk with the professionals such as attorneys and CPA's, as these advisors will advise entrepreneurs when it comes to selecting a business entity (Hertz et al., 2009).

The first part of the literature review looked at general business entity selection, as well as some of the things that the entrepreneur needs to look at when making the selection of an entity (Baik et al., 2015). Entrepreneurs need to think, not just about their needs today, but the needs that the business might have in a few years, such as seeking venture capital (Estabrook, 2009). Taxes are always a key factor, but that also needs to include state and local taxes as well as Federal (Donohoe et al., 2015).

The first entity that was looked at in detail was the S corporation. The S corporation starts out as a C corporation, but files Form 2553, and elects to be taxed as an S corporation with the IRS (Alberty, 2003). What makes this selection unique is that the entity now has pass-through taxation, as opposed to a separate entity tax (Burton & Karlinsky, 2007). Because the regulations governing the S corporation are under a different section of the tax code, S corporations offer some unique features that the other pass-through entities do not offer (Hodder et al., 2003).

The next entity to be looked at was the LLC, which is created by state statute, and started in Wyoming (Cleveland et al., 1996). Most states enacted their own LLC legislation in the first half of the 1990s, and the LLC has been gaining in popularity since then (Chrisman, 2010). It offers the limited liability that the two corporations offer, but it is more flexible without many of the formalities of the corporations (Banoff & Lipton, 2003). It also offers flexibility in how it will be managed. The LLC can either be a pass-through entity, like the S corporation, or it can be taxed like a C corporation.

The differences between the LLC and the S corporation were the next things to be looked at. The LLC does not have the ownership restrictions that the S corporation does, nor does it have the formalities, such as shareholder meetings that the S corporation does have (Petravick & Troutman, 2007). The LLC also does not have the passive income limitations that the S corporation has, but the S corporation has a few benefits when it comes to paying the owners, who are actively running the business (Schatz et al., 1996). One final disadvantage for the LLC is that since it is relatively new, there are still many unanswered questions that will need to be addressed through a court case, changes in the laws, and other regulatory changes (Johnson, 2015).

After looking at a few up and coming entities, most of which are a variation on the LLC, the gaps in the literature were looked at (Bahena, 2010). The first gap is the misunderstanding by entrepreneurs as well as many professionals when it comes to limited liability (Misenti, 2016). The other gap was in the perception of the C corporation, which many see as an entity with double taxation, and little else, when most entrepreneurs do not pay the double taxation, and instead receive many write-offs that the others cannot receive (Raible et al., 2015).

The last area to be looked at was the conceptual framework, which not only offered a visual to how the business entity selection process should go, but also showed what can happen when things do not go as planned, or when this field of study is not properly understood by entrepreneurs or their advisors (Opiela, 2004). It ended with a few questions that need to be addressed regarding business entity selection (Treusch, 2003).

In the next chapter, some of the questions that have emerged from a review of the literature will be addressed. Hopefully, some of them can be answered, and information can be provided that can help future entrepreneurs avoid some of the mistakes that today's entrepreneurs have made.

CHAPTER THREE

The problem that was addressed in the study is the strategies business managers need to establish an organizational structure appropriate for entrepreneurial business operations. In 2015, there were approximately 680,000 new business startups, creating 3 million new jobs (Statistics, 2018). Selecting the wrong business entity for an entrepreneur's situation could cause the business to fail, instead of succeeding (Baik et al., 2015). By clearing up some of the misconceptions about business entities, which are prevalent in the literature, entrepreneurs, and their advisors can have a better understanding of the selection process, and what the needs of the entrepreneur are (Blair & Marcum, 2015).

The purpose of this qualitative research was to explore the strategies business managers need to establish an organizational structure appropriate for entrepreneurial business operations. The business managers were interviewed to learn from their experiences and gain a better understanding of how they established an organizational structure. This exploratory study specifically looked at 8 business managers in Tulsa County, Oklahoma to learn from their shared experiences in establishing an entrepreneurial business organizational structure.

This chapter will be a look at the research tradition and design. It will also explore the population for this study, and how the sampling procedure was selected. It will end with a look at the instrumentation and the validity and reliability of the data that will be collected and analyzed.

Research Tradition

A methodology is used in research to collect information and data in order to study and understand a problem (Creswell, 1998). The methodology dictates how the data is collected, what kind of data is collected, and how it is analyzed (Converse, 2012). There are three methodologies used in research; qualitative, quantitative, and mixed methods, which uses a combination of the first two.

The qualitative methodology was used for the study. A qualitative study is used to advance an understanding of fundamental reasons, opinions, and motivations (Hennink et al., 2011). A qualitative methodology provides insights into a problem, helps to develop ideas or hypotheses for future quantitative study (Thomas et al., 2015).

The qualitative method was the best approach for this research as it looks to understand and explore a particular social and human problem (Creswell, 1998). The quantitative methodology was not used for the study because this study was not building on previous work and was more exploratory in nature (Converse, 2012). The mixed methods methodology was not used for the study because the mixed methods is a combination of the qualitative and quantitative, and this study was best served with a purely qualitative method (Thomas et al., 2015).

A research design is used to elaborate on what the population that is of interest to the researcher is, what sample size will be studied, and how the sample will be selected (Thomas et al., 2015). The research design also discusses how the sample will be studied, what instruments will be needed to study the sample, as well as how the data will be analyzed (Hennink et al., 2011). The research design is the outline that will detail how the group will be studied (Converse, 2012).

Based on the selection of the qualitative methodology, an exploratory design approach was used (Converse, 2012). An exploratory research design was the best fit to answer the research question, as the design is looking at exploring the experiences of the participants (Tomkins, 2013). The purpose was to study the experiences of those business managers and their selection of a business entity in the Tulsa, Oklahoma area, which was best served with an exploratory design.

An exploratory qualitative approach was appropriate for the study because this study was interested in exploring the experiences of the participants (Converse, 2012). The researcher considered three design options: ethnography, case study, and grounded theory. The case study design was not used for the study because the case study is focused on a specific company or event. The ethnography design was not used in the study because the research was not served best by the researcher being immersed into an organization. The grounded theory design was not used in the study because a grounded theory has many more participants and is more concerned with developing theory and not about exploring the participant's experiences (Tomkins, 2013).

Research Question

The research question for this research was: What are the strategies business managers need to establish an organizational structure appropriate for entrepreneurial business operations?

Research Design

The research design refers to the overall strategy that integrates the different components of the study in a coherent and logical way, thereby, ensuring the research problem will be effectively addressed (Converse, 2012). The research design constitutes the blueprint for the collection, measurement, and analysis of data (Shenton, 2004). The research design is organized by population and sample, sampling procedure, instrumentation, validity, reliability, data collection, data analysis, and ethical considerations.

Population and Sample

The population in a research study is a group of people that share a common characteristic that the researcher is interested in studying (Thomas et al., 2015). The population for this study were business managers, in the Tulsa, Oklahoma area that have successfully established organizational structures for entrepreneurial business operations. The estimated size of the population is 60,000. This population is appropriate because approximately 12% of adults are starting or in the process of starting a new business, and the adult population of Tulsa County is approximately 490,000 (Kelley et al., 2017).

A sample is a part of the population that will actually be looked at, but the sample should represent the entire population (Hennink et al., 2011). Sample size is the number of participants that is needed to accurately represent the population and seek saturation (Thomas et al., 2015). The sample size was 8 business managers (Hertz et al., 2009). The sample size is appropriate because Creswell (1998) and Thomas, et al. (2015) have stated that the sample size is within the appropriate size for an exploratory study

Sampling Procedure

A sampling procedure is a process by which the sample is selected (Creswell, 1998). For the study, purposeful sampling was used as the sampling procedure. Purposeful sampling allows participants to be targeted, and it can produce an in-depth insight and understanding of the research question and the purpose of the study (Thomas et al., 2015). Purposeful sampling was appropriate for the study because the participants could be targeted, as opposed to random sampling (Tomkins, 2013).

Potential participants were selected using LinkedIn, to find individuals that met the criteria of this study. Potential participants were contacted after IRB approval, using emails or phone numbers obtained from LinkedIn. Participants are characterized by establishing selection criteria (Tracy, 2013). The required demographic characteristics are not applicable in this study, as the researcher was more concerned with the participants' professional background for this study.

Potential participants were contacted by email or phone requesting their participation. When a participant agreed to participate in the study, the informed consent form (see Appendix A) was sent to the participant (Thomas et al., 2015). Next, interview times and dates were established with each study participant.

Instrumentation

For qualitative research, the researcher is an implicit part of the research and must collect valid and reliable data (Creswell, 1998). Qualitative researchers often serve as the instrument (Tracy, 2013). Qualitative research uses open-ended questions in order to acquire more detail than a simple yes or no.

During data collection, a voice recorder was used to capture data from face-to-face interviews. The interview process used interview questions to capture the interviewee's perceptions (see Appendix B). The interviews lasted 45-60 minutes. A semi-structured interview with open-ended questions was chosen to allow for a more natural conversation as opposed to an interrogation style of interview (Rubin & Rubin, 2005). The participants were also be more likely to feel comfortable sharing their experiences on the topic if it is more of a conversation about the topic, as opposed to only being able to answer particular questions on the topic. This type of interview also allows for the use of follow up questions to explain better their experiences on the subject.

In the interview protocol template, a digital voice recorder, and laptop were the primary data collection tools for the study (Rubin & Rubin, 2005). The voice recorder was a tablet, which allowed instant encryption of the recording once it was finished, and the answers were typed into a laptop, using Microsoft Word, to also allow instant encryption. The researcher took note of any observations, such as the participant's facial expressions when giving an answer or other expressions or emotions that were displayed.

Open-ended, semi-structured interview questions were used to explore the participant's experiences with business entity selection. Creswell (1998) noted open-ended interview questions encourage participants to provide detailed descriptions of their experiences. Depending on the responses provided, follow-up or probing questions were used to capture additional details (Rubin & Rubin, 2005). One-on-one interviews took place at a date and time of convenient to each participant.

Validity

Validity is the appropriateness of the tools, processes, and data (Creswell, 1998). Validity is important for a qualitative study because it shows that the research question, methods, tools, and data were the best choices for studying the phenomenon (Thomas et al., 2015). Validity was demonstrated by the study being dependable, credible, transferable, and confirmable (Shenton, 2004).

Dependability is the reliability or ability to replicate the findings in a similar study (Tracy, 2013). Dependability is important for a qualitative study because it adds to the legitimacy of the findings, as future researchers could replicate the study with similar findings (Shenton, 2004). For the study, dependability was addressed by addressing any unusual occurrences that might be found in the study that could make it harder for future researchers to replicate this study. Outliers that are found in this study might not apply to future studies and would need to be explained, so that future researchers understand what the outliers were and why they happened.

Credibility is the believability and trustworthiness of the findings (Creswell, 1998). Credibility is important for a qualitative study because it reflects the richness of the data, and the participants feel that the data truly reflects the phenomenon that is being studied (Shenton, 2004). For this study, credibility was addressed by using member checking, which is sharing the data and proposed findings of this study with the participants, so the participants can determine if the results truly reflect the feelings and thoughts of the participants. Member checking ensures there are no misconceptions or misunderstandings between the researcher, the participants and the data that was collected.

Transferability is the ease at which the results can be transferred to other contexts (Tracy, 2013). Transferability is important for a qualitative study because the results can be applied to similar populations (Shenton, 2004). For this study, transferability was addressed by clearly describing the context of the research, including the assumptions that were made, so that the reader will understand the context of this research, and will be able to make their own judgments on how to transfer the results to a different context.

Confirmability is the measure of the objectivity used in evaluating the results (Hennink et al., 2011). Confirmability is important for a qualitative study because the findings need to be backed up by the actual data, and not what the researcher would like the findings to be (Shenton, 2004). For this study, confirmability was addressed by letting others look at the data and see if the same results are reached that the researcher found. This can include professors, other researchers, or even the participants.

Reliability

Reliability relates to the ability of a measuring instrument to accurately and consistently show the same result (Creswell, 1998). Reliability refers to the extent of the consistency of the instrumentation being used in the study (Shenton, 2004).

Reliability is the consistency with which researchers measure the results of an instrument accurately and consistently (Tracy, 2013). Triangulation improves the reliability of collected data by using more than more than one data source (Shenton, 2004). The reliability of the collected data obtained by asking open-ended questions increases the reliability of the data and triangulation (Thomas et al., 2015).

Conducting member checking enhances the reliability and validity of the data collection process (Shenton, 2004). After reviewing the interview data, the researcher provided a copy to the participants to make sure that the data accurately represented their thoughts and feelings on the subject. Researchers use member checking to validate study findings (Hennink et al., 2011).

Using triangulation contributes to the richness of the study and also deepens and widens the understanding (Shenton, 2004). Through triangulation, the researcher identified categories and themes using multiple resources. Triangulation is a data analysis technique used in qualitative case studies to check and establish validity (Hennink et al., 2011). Triangulation is the process of using multiple methods of data to develop a comprehensive understanding of the phenomena (Rubin & Rubin, 2005). For this study, triangulation was accomplished by recording and transcribing the interviews, which contains the researcher's interpretations and participant's intentions, was compared to the interview notes (Tomkins, 2013). The participants were also provided a copy of the transcribed data to validate that the data matches their intended answers.

A pilot study was conducted by interviewing a member of the population. The pilot study tested the survey instrumentation to verify that the questions performed as expected in extracting the appropriate data (Converse, 2012). The results of the pilot study did not become a part of the final research (Rubin & Rubin, 2005).

Data Collection

The research question guides the data collection process necessary to capture needed information for the study (Creswell, 1998). The research question was: What are the strategies business managers need to establish an organizational structure appropriate for entrepreneurial business operations? The data collection technique selected to answer the research question was semi-structured interviews. Semi-structured interviews provide reliable data, in-depth answers, and the opportunity for follow up questions to elaborate on an answer (Rubin & Rubin, 2005). Semi-structured interviews encourage participants to elaborate on their experiences (Thomas et al., 2015).

Phone and email were used to communicate with participants to confirm their willingness to participate and coordinate their availability. Participants also received the researcher's email and phone number. Communication via email and phone was used with participants until the interviews were completed.

Eight business administrators/ entrepreneurs were interviewed. As specified in the interview protocol (see Appendix C), participants were asked open-ended questions and follow-up questions during the semi-structured interviews. The interviews were conducted at their offices. The exact location, date, and time of each interview was established after confirming participation.

Each interview included the following general process: (a) establish rapport with the participant; (b) introduce the study, its purpose, and its constraints; (c) obtain a signed consent agreement form (see Appendix A), (d) use the interview protocol (see Appendix C) to ensure all questions are asked and are in the correct format, (e) use probing techniques of the silent probe, overt encouragement, elaboration, clarification, and reflection; (f) thank the participant for their time and efforts.

Interviews were recorded using voice recording software on a tablet. A laptop was used during the interview to capture some key thoughts, as well as non-verbal cues that the participants give.

After the interviews were completed, the recorded information was transcribed to Microsoft Word using a laptop. This process involved recording their answers from the voice recorder to the appropriate file, to be coded.

The collected data to be stored includes the voice recordings, the transcriptions of the recordings, and the digital notes that were recorded. These data will be stored for 5 years on a flash drive in a secure location.

In summary, data collection occurred using notes, recordings of interviews, and observations of study participants (Tomkins, 2013). Each interview took 45-60 minutes and was recorded. The recorded data was transcribed in MS Word and password protected. The data was then cross-referenced with any notes and relevant information that was collected (Rubin & Rubin, 2005).

The data collection began before the interview questions were asked. Once the participants had been selected, the participants were provided with an introduction to the study to see if the participants were interested in participating (Thomas et al., 2015). This also included how the interview would be recorded, to make sure that the participants were comfortable with it. Before the participants could participate, the participants reviewed and signed an informed consent form.

Each participant was asked the same initial questions, allowing time for them to answer the question, before adding any follow-up questions thoroughly. Once all of the questions had been asked, the participants were allowed to add any thoughts they might have on the topic, as this could be an area for future research, or the participants had something pertinent, but it never came up in a question.

Data Analysis

An exploratory qualitative methodology was selected over other qualitative designs because the focus of the research is to categorize and interpret themes (Tomkins, 2013). Qualitative data analysis methods are conceptual and relational (Thomas et al., 2015). Conceptual data analysis involves establishes the presence of themes. Relational data analysis begins with the identification of present concepts and continues by looking for semantic relationships (Tracy, 2013). Semantic relationships are established using thematic units. Thematic units are high-level abstractions interpreted from basic themes and patterns established in the qualitative data (Shenton, 2004).

Data analysis process involves the emergence of themes from the interview transcripts and other collected data, such as the personal journal (Tomkins, 2013). Descriptive coding was used in the coding of the data (Saldana, 2016). In this method, the researcher looks for keywords that highlight the experiences of the interviewee. Tools, such as conditional formatting in Microsoft Word, were used to highlight these keywords if they are present among the other interviews.

Data analysis begins by organizing the collected information followed by data perusal, classification, and synthesis (Shenton, 2004). The data analysis approach for exploratory analysis includes (a) compiling the data from the interviews, (b) organizing the data by interviewee, (c) coding of the data (i.e., organizing the data by recognized categories), (d) identifying themes (i.e., the label attached to each recognized category), and (e) establishing data relationships (i.e., recognizing similarities and differences in themes in order to condense or separate themed categories, as appropriate) (Thomas et al., 2015). Once this process was completed, the established themed categories are the findings of the study.

The coding rules that were used to map textual units into data terms will be descriptive coding (Saldana, 2016). In descriptive coding a word or phrase is assigned that summarizes the main topic of a passage (Miles, Huberman, & Saldana, 2014). These codes provide an inventory of topics that highlight the data that was collected.

The technique that was used to translate data terms into themes was comparing the codes from one data set or interview with others (Saldana, 2016). As similar codes were found in multiple interviews, those represented commonalities that multiple participants expressed and became themes in the research (Miles et al., 2014).

The themes and combinations of themes were recorded in Microsoft Excel for further analysis to see which themes were predominate throughout the study (Tracy, 2013). Conditional formatting in Microsoft Word was also be used to highlight codes and themes from interview and compare it to other interviews to see if those codes were present as well (Tomkins, 2013).

Ethical Considerations

The ethical ideologies that applied throughout the research process included receiving an informed consent, which apprised the participants of the right to a safe atmosphere for the interview (see Appendix A), and informing the participant of the right to terminate the interview for any reason (Hennink et al., 2011). A signed informed consent was signed before the interview can begin.

Ideologies of the Belmont Report were upheld in order to ensure the highest level of ethical research. The Belmont Report values are primarily focused on the well-being of study subjects (Thomas et al., 2015). The susceptible research population must be protected from potential misuse (Tomkins, 2013). Also, the three principles of the Belmont Report protocol (i.e., autonomy, beneficence, and justice) were maintained

Researchers must ensure no maltreatment comes to participants due to participation in a study (Thomas et al., 2015). Risks must also be minimalized to participants. To ensure consciousness of the hazards and benefits of the study, each participant was required to sign an informed consent form (see Appendix A). The consent form includes (a) the purpose of the study, (b) the involvement of participates, (c) participation procedures, (d) the benefits of the research, (e) the risks of taking part, (f) costs and compensation, (g) confidentiality, (h) voluntary nature of participating, and (i) the rights of the participant to withdraw (Rubin & Rubin, 2005).

Biases could occur due to preexisting knowledge and experience with the topic (Creswell, 1998). Bias were mitigated by using open-ended questions during the interview, focusing solely on the responses of participants, performing triangulation, and using note taking.

Summary of Chapter Three

This chapter was a look at the research methods for this particular study, which was a qualitative study with an exploratory design. This design was selected to explore the experiences of business administrators in establishing an entrepreneurial business organizational structure (Tomkins, 2013).

The researcher purposely selected a sample of 8 business managers for this study. The instrumentation for this research study was a semi-structured interview consisting of several open-ended questions, allowing for follow-up questions to further expand on the participant's answers.

Validity and reliability were ensured through asking each participant the same open-ended questions, as a way of making sure everyone received the same information and any differences in their answers will be based solely on different experiences and not on being asked different questions.

Chapter 4 will be a look at the data that was collected during this study, as well as information about the participants. The themes that emerged as part of the data analysis will also be looked at in chapter 4.

CHAPTER FOUR

The purpose of the qualitative exploratory study was to explore the strategies business managers need to establish an organizational structure appropriate for entrepreneurial business operations. The researcher used a qualitative method with an exploratory design to collect data on the experiences of entrepreneurs with a focus on strategies that are needed to establish an organizational structure. Qualitative interviews took place with research participants, which provided data from the experiences of the participants. This research design is used when the researcher's approach is to ascertain and create theory. Chapter 4 provides a brief overview of the demographics of the participants, a detailed presentation of the data, and a presentation and discussion of the findings.

Participant Demographics

The participants for this study are shown in Table 1, along with some demographics that are relevant to this study. While the focus of this study was entrepreneurs, the researcher also wanted input from experts to give background information that could be compared to the information provided by the entrepreneurs, as a way of adding another layer of depth to the findings.

Table 1

Participant Demographics

Participant	Gender	Occupation/ Industry	Type of Business
1	M	CPA	N/A
2	M	Counselor	LLC
3	F	Counselor	LLC
4	F	Home Daycare	LLC

5	F	Photographer	Sole Proprietorship
6	M	Multiple Businesses	Sole Proprietorship
7	M	Learning Systems	LLC
8	M	Web Design	Sole Proprietorship

Presentation of the Data

Each of the participants was asked the same set of questions, which can be found in the Appendix. What follows are the answers to the questions, but it is not all inclusive of everything that was said. The answers represent the key thoughts and ideas that the participants expressed during the interviews.

Participant 1

The first participant will be Male, who is a CPA.

1. One of the strategies in establishing an organizational structure is understanding the needs of the entrepreneur in terms of what an organizational structure can provide. Can you describe the factors or characteristics that an entrepreneur should consider when selecting a legal organizational structure?

I think the first thing an entrepreneur should consider regarding their organizational structure is tax filing status. Failure to understand the income tax consequences of operating as a sole proprietorship, pass through entity (partnership, LLC, S-corporation), or a C-corporation can result in the loss of personal assets by creditors, lengthy and expensive legal proceedings with other stakeholders, or underpayment of tax liabilities. All of the above can easily lead to the voluntary of forced dissolution of the entrepreneur's small business, which have a high failure rate due to these factors amongst others. The second thing the entrepreneur should consider from a legal standpoint is the Corporate by-laws. Specifically, who will own the shares, voting rights, and governance of the entity. In the event of litigation, the entrepreneur's corporate by-laws should support the mission of the business and limit the liability for acts committed by employees or other stakeholders of the business.

2. What are the most significant characteristics to consider when deciding on an organizational structure?

The first thing I think should be considered in establishing organizational structure is the entrepreneur's role in the operation of the business, and the way those beneath him/her should be arranged. With this comes defined roles, a lack of which can result in discontent among employees if the entrepreneur feels the need to micro-manage the day to day operations of the business, which should not happen if he/she has hired qualified employees and managers. I believe the most successful entrepreneurs spend the majority of their time building brand equity with customers, and planning and executing strategy for the direction of the business while leaving the day-to-day operations to qualified managers and employees. To take it a step further, I believe corporate org charts should be structured and detailed with a clear chain of command in place. The entrepreneur should also make sure he/she has done everything in their power to set everyone in the organization up for success, rather directly or indirectly through support provided to managers to empower them to set the employees up for success."

4. One aspect that attracts people to forming an organization structure is limited liability. How well do you think entrepreneurs understand what liability is limited and what is not?

I do not believe most entrepreneurs understand legal liability without proper legal assistance.

a. Do you think that having proper insurance would help in reducing liability?

I think having proper insurance is essential to reducing liability. I believe it is best summed up in the phrase *you don't know what you need, until you need it*. The average entrepreneur is not likely to know the areas his/her business will be at risk for legal liability, so they should due their due diligence to seek out legal counsel that specialize in this area, and ensures they have the right amount of insurance.

b. For clarification, will you elaborate on limited liability?

Limited liability is primarily applicable to organizations with more than one shareholder. It is designed to protect the entity, and its shareholders, from acts committed by shareholders that could put the business at risk for litigation. It also limits shareholder liability for claims by creditors against personal assets in the event of default by limiting such claims to the assets of the business.

5. What are some aspects or characteristics that many entrepreneurs are focusing too much time on?

I believe out of network marketing is the area entrepreneurs spend too much time focusing on. While I do believe it is extremely important to establish your presence in the business community, the most successful marketing is done through the entrepreneurs' immediate and extended network, often through LinkedIn, instead of advertising to unknown customers at various events and locations.

a. Why do you think that entrepreneurs are focusing so much on these?

Desire for expedited growth.

b. Tell me how this can be changed?

Maximization of marketing to indiduals in your own network, and encouraging them to reach out to those in their networks; identifying events where the marketing can occur by speaking to a crowd so people do not feel like they are being targeted/harassed.

6. What are some aspects or characteristics that many entrepreneurs are either ignoring or spending too little time on?

Core values of their company.

a. Why do you think that these areas are being ignored?

Entrepreneuars often pledge their personal assets as collateral for loans needed to start their business, so their time if spent on growing the business as much as possible.

b. Tell me how this can be changed?

Having a clearly defined set of core values foundational to the organization's success and direction before applying for a start-up loan.

7. Tell me about the research you performed before selecting an organizational structure?

N/A-I am not an entrepreneur, but I believe pass through entity's are the best organization structure because you avoid double taxation issues C-corporations face, and your personal assets are often protected from creditor claims whereas they are not under sole proprietorship structures.

Participant 2

The second participant will be Male, who is a family counselor. He originally started out part time as a sole proprietor in the evenings but moved to full time when the hospital closed down the behavioral health division. The participant had some issues when converting the practice into the LLC, such as with insurance. He chose the LLC primarily for the reason of limited liability. He did not know much about what limited liability was, but knew it was important to have. His knowledge of the LLC came primarily from a business partner from another business venture. This partner advised an LLC for their venture and for the counseling venture as well. Recommended the LLC be set up in Nevada as it offered more protection than what could be found domestically in Oklahoma. When asked if he could go back and do anything differently the participant stated that he wished he could have set up the LLC from the beginning instead of starting out as a Sole Proprietor.

Participant 3

The third participant will be Female who is a counselor.

7. Tell me about the research you performed before selecting an organizational structure?

A lot of starting out with my own practice has been a learning curve. I have done some research but then also feel like I have been flying by the seat of pants to some extent as well. I decided to open an LLC because it was my understanding that that would protect my personal assets if things were to go poorly with my practice. I chose to do an LLC rather than a PLLC for a couple of reasons: (a) I filed my LLC online and wasn't sure how to do that with a PLLC and (b) I thought the LLC rather than the PLLC left me with more options in case I ever wanted to do just consulting rather than clinical therapy. The research I did was online through OK Commerce and Secretary of State.

9. What, if anything, would you change about your decision on selecting a legal entity if you could?

I still consider my knowledge to be rather limited and am learning on a daily basis. Had I known what I know now when I started, I would have stayed in my part-time job a little longer to give myself some more cushion while building up my business. I am a Licensed Clinical Social Worker and work primarily with older adults who are struggling with depression and anxiety. I bill insurance and did not realize how long it would take to become credentialed on various insurance panels. I also think it would have been easier to connect with an accountant and insurance biller earlier than I did. I have since hired both and it has decreased my stress significantly.

10. What other items should be added to our discussion?

My advice to future entrepreneurs who aren't business majors would be to do research and meet with others who have similar businesses to learn from their experience. Not sure this is possible for everyone, but in my line of business it makes sense.

Participant 4

Participant 4 is Female, who has a home daycare.

7. Tell me about the research you performed before selecting an organizational structure?

I set up an LLC for liability purposes. I wanted my personal assets unaffected in the event of a lawsuit by a client. My husband had done extensive research, both online and from speaking with businessmen, and decided an LLC was the fit for me.

9. What, if anything, would you change about your decision on selecting a legal entity if you could?

If I could go back, I probably would stay a DBA. An LLC has A LOT of paperwork to keep track of for the IRS. All ducks need to be in a row and all spending justified.

Participant 5

Participant 5 is Female, who is a photographer.

7. Tell me about the research you performed before selecting an organizational structure?

I did hundreds of hours of research before starting my official business. I joined entrepreneur Facebook groups started following entrepreneurs on Instagram and downloaded

Podcasts from successful business people. I had been doing photography casually for a few years and when I was ready to start my business, I headed to YouTube to see how! It has been hard to learn the ins and outs of business when I do not have a background in it, BUT there are so many online resources now that really anyone with enough vision and drive can learn!

9. What, if anything, would you change about your decision on selecting a legal entity if you could?

I think if I could go back, I would have gone to school for business; however, it is possible that in the near future I will go back for my business degree.

10. What other items should be added to our discussion?

Advice: I would say, be bullheaded about your dreams. If it is something that you really want, you will take the time to learn how to do it, even if you do not have any experience or knowledge about it. I would say surround yourself with people who believe in what you're doing because from day to day the temptation to give up comes but having people around you who support you help you to keep going after your dreams!

Participant 6

Participant 6 will be Male, who has multiple businesses.

1. One of the strategies in establishing an organizational structure is understanding the needs of the entrepreneur in terms of what an organizational structure can provide. Can you describe the factors or characteristics that an entrepreneur should consider when selecting a legal organizational structure?

In considering an organizational structure one should first ask, what could I lose if I choose the wrong structure, the second is what is going to make the business the most profit considering controllable aspects. Such as, I can control the costs of production if its a product, I can control the price I sell my product for, what I cannot control are the laws that allow the governing bodies in my State and Country to reach into my profit margin and thereby effect my ability to employ people, help my family and investing giving into my community. By choosing the right legal structure I can decide how my business will be viewed by those governing bodies.

    a. Tell me more about why these should be considered?

        No one can predict with 100% accuracy the future of the economy they will be conducting business in. Understanding that there are uncontrollable aspects, the legal structure should be flexible to allow for change yet provide protection at the same time.

    b. What are the most significant characteristics to consider when deciding on an organizational structure?

        Someone must be the final word on what is and is not going to be accomplished; who reports to whom and when.

    c. Tell me more about why these are the most important to consider?

        This person is responsible not only for every person within the organization in regard to insuring the various tasks are accomplished, they are also responsible to report to the applicable government agencies information required, thereby allowing them to remain identified as the legal structure chosen for the company.

4. One aspect that attracts people to forming an organization structure is limited liability. How well do you think entrepreneurs understand what liability is limited and what is not?

When I started my company, I understood I was liable for every aspect of the business. What I did not understand is the degree that would impact my life.

    a. Do you think that having proper insurance would help in reducing liability?

The purpose of insurance is to shift the financial liability, it does not shift liability in the event of an illegal act on the part of the business officers.

    b. For clarification, will you elaborate on limited liability?

Limiting liability allows for the personal assets of the officers to be free from certain seizers by those with legal suits against the corporation.

5. What are some aspects or characteristics that many entrepreneurs are focusing too much time on?

In my case, I focused more on production instead of sales. Although production is essential, sales was the future of, and sustainability of the company.

    a. Why do you think that entrepreneurs are focusing so much on these?

It is what they are most comfortable with.

    b. Tell me how this can be changed?

An understanding that in the beginning you must have an ability to do all aspects of the business or the resources to hire someone to do them for you. It is noteworthy that this could affect the legal structure, in that possibly no one would be willing to just be an employee for that function and require you to make them a business partner. In that case, a decision would need to be made as to whether to change the approach.

6. What are some aspects or characteristics that many entrepreneurs are either ignoring or spending too little time on?

Writing a business plan that will work. Just because a person may know the mechanics of a business plan doesn't mean they have a workable plan. Having it looked over by an account, multiple business owners that you trust, and a lawyer are in my opinion a good investment of your time and finances.

    a. Why do you think that these areas are being ignored?

        A number of reasons, one is excitement; wanting to be the first to implement your business idea. In my opinion, the number one reason is pride. We seem to estimate our knowledge as infinite when the reality is, it is finite.

    b. Tell me how this can be changed?

        Sometimes we learn more from a failure than we do from a success. Interview not only those who got it right, but also those who got it wrong. There is much to be learned from both.

7. Do you feel you adequately prepared?

I heard it said that preparation time is never wasted time. There is also the time to get out and get it done. I feel more prepared now than I did when I first started my business. At least now I am not going into business with unrealistic beliefs.

    a. Tell me more about why you feel you either did or did not?

        There were so many things I was unprepared for in the beginning. I understood all the mechanical aspects of the business; what I failed at was believing other people were going to honor their contracts, and that quality would produce more clients.

8. What are some of the aspects or characteristics that you looked at or considered when you created an organizational structure?

What are the tasks that I am weakest in and staff those weaknesses.

    a. What was important?

        In retrospect, what can I do and what are the things I cannot do.

9. What, if anything, would you change about your decision on selecting a legal entity if you could?

I was the sole owner with no other considerations. In that instance, I would have taken on a partner and created a Limited Partnership.

    a. Why would you change this?

To cover my weaknesses and make the business more profitable.

Participant 7

Participant 7 will be Male, who creates learning systems.

1. One of the strategies in establishing an organizational structure is understanding the needs of the entrepreneur in terms of what an organizational structure can provide. Can you describe the factors or characteristics that an entrepreneur should consider when selecting a legal organizational structure?

In my experience the most important consideration for a small, growing business is: What will get you off the ground the fastest? The number one factor for me in choosing to be a single-member LLC was that it is the simplest structure for a small business to set up. My organizational structure provides limited liability so that I am protected in the case of a law suit, but I can still treat the business's income as personal income and do my taxes in almost the same way I did as an employee or contractor. It is essential to choose an organizational structure, but instead of belaboring what would be optimal 10 years in the future, I chose the structure that worked immediately and then simply started working on getting business.

    a. Tell me more about why these should be considered?

Small businesses need an easy way to get off the ground quickly. Unless there is expectation of hiring dozens of salaried employees in the first year or two, or of reporting profit and loss to third parties, a simple LLC does the trick for hitting the ground running.

2. What are the most significant characteristics to consider when deciding on an organizational structure?

Coming at this from the perspective of an online business, I would recommend other business owners in a similar position to ensure that they are doing everything legally; they should consider an organizational structure based on what their mentors and accountant recommend in order to sleep well at night.

a. Tell me more about why these are the most important to consider?

Many of the entrepreneurs that I know actually began as subcontractors and grew from there. We are very used to working for ourselves, filing personal taxes, and doing all the things that a subcontractor would do. From there, business begins to do well, and we start to delegate responsibilities and grow quickly. But as we begin to hire contractors of our own, or full time employees, it is tempting to continue doing our paperwork in a business-as-usual fashion; however, once we begin expanding into such entrepreneurial territory, it's important to recognize where we are and look for advice (from mentors and accountants) on making sure our structural status makes sense, legally and financially.

3. What are the least significant characteristics to consider?

Taxation details that make a very small difference to the bottom line. From the perspective of a small business with 10 contractors and no W-2 employees, I think that trying to choose a structure that optimizes taxation to the final 1% or 2% can be a vain endeavor. For example, in my opinion there is little reason to consider a C-corp at this stage if it makes very little difference in the final profit, unless rapid growth is expected in the near future.

    a. Tell me more about why these are the least important to consider?

        An entrepreneur who is in the driver seat of a small business needs to focus on operations, sales, and systematic growth. We have limited attention. In many cases, the attention that it takes to optimize taxation benefits to the final 1% could have been used to create 20% more revenue in new sales! That doesn't make sense mathematically. Of course, optimizing the organizational structure for taxes has a place; that point will probably come after the entrepreneur.

4. One aspect that attracts people to forming an organization structure is limited liability. How well do you think entrepreneurs understand what liability is limited and what is not?

In my experience as a virtual (internet-based) business, many business owners, even with dozens of contractors, do not think much about limited liability. Again, this is coming from my own experience, but most of the entrepreneurs that I know hardly consider it since they have very few channels through which they are likely to affect an entity in such a way that makes them liable to a law suit.

    a. Do you think that having proper insurance would help in reducing liability?

        This is possible, but my own business has an extremely low chance of being subject to lawsuits, so I have never considered insurance for my business.

5. What are some aspects or characteristics that many entrepreneurs are focusing too much time on?

There are some entrepreneurs who spend too much time trying to choose an organizational structure that will work 10 years down the road when they could simply choose a working option and moving along from there.

    a. Why do you think that entrepreneurs are focusing so much on these?

        Many entrepreneurs are very detail-oriented and want to understand every nut and bolt of their business and their finances; this is a good quality to have, but it is impossible to plan for every contingency and some things are better left to experts, for example depending on an accountant that you can trust who specializes in their type of business.

    b. Tell me how this can be changed?

        Probably the best way this could be changed would be through hiring accountants who specialize in the organization's own way of doing business. For example, I would love to have an accountant who has extensive experience with online businesses similar to mine! But, such specialist accountants are difficult to find.

6. What are some aspects or characteristics that many entrepreneurs are either ignoring or spending too little time on?

Many of the entrepreneurs that I know spend too little time considering how their organizational structure affects their profit and loss over time. It is tempting to choose an organizational structure and simply stick with it for several years, but as the business grows, restructuring is very often a good idea in order to optimize income/profit vs. tax. For example, an LLC is great for getting started as a solopreneur who hires contractors, but as revenue grows, a C-corp becomes more attractive for the tax advantages.

    a. Why do you think that these areas are being ignored?

>Many entrepreneurs spend so much time inside the business, running day-to-day operations and sales, that they fail to step back and consider the math of how the business's structure affects the bottom line.

b. Tell me how this can be changed?

>Entrepreneurs should consult their accountants regularly not just for routine purposes, but to reconsider their organizational structure on at least a yearly basis.

7. Tell me about the research you performed before selecting an organizational structure?

>My research came down to seeing what my own business mentors recommended, doing some simple online searches to confirm that it seemed to make sense, and following in their footsteps.

a. Do you feel you adequately prepared?

>Yes and no: I feel quite comfortable with what my business has done to this point, but as we are in a period of rapid growth, I feel a need to reconsider and do much more research and preparation for dealing with the higher profits in order to optimize our after-tax bottom line.

b. Tell me more about why you feel you either did or did not?

>At the beginning, I felt very comfortable with my organizational structure because I could essentially treat my business as a contracting entity with subcontractors; all my taxes were personal income taxes, which I was comfortable with at the time.

8. What are some of the aspects or characteristics that you looked at or considered when you created an organizational structure?

In my case, I knew many other business owners who had very similar businesses to mine, so my default response was simply to choose the same organizational structure that they chose (single-member LLC) and then not worry beyond that.

    a. What was important?

        My primary consideration was that I was doing business legally and could get started on operations/sales/marketing without worrying that I would be shut down.

    b. What was not important?

        I did not consider optimization of the tax benefits of the different organizational structures, as I simply wanted to begin doing business.

9. What, if anything, would you change about your decision on selecting a legal entity if you could?

I probably could have benefited from understanding the different organizational structures a little bit better.

    a. Why would you change this?

        It probably would not have changed my decision, but I might have been a little more confident in my choice and I might have had some vision for when it might be a good idea (a few years down the road) to restructure.

Participant 8

Participant 8 will be Male, who is in web development.

1. One of the strategies in establishing an organizational structure is understanding the needs of the entrepreneur in terms of what an organizational structure can provide. Can you

describe the factors or characteristics that an entrepreneur should consider when selecting a legal organizational structure?

Type of industry, degree of legal risk to personal assets, potential corporate tax benefits.

2. What are the most significant characteristics to consider when deciding on an organizational structure?

Who is involved, how much they have at stake, how much ownership to allot each, how to divide responsibilities.

4. One aspect that attracts people to forming an organization structure is limited liability. How well do you think entrepreneurs understand what liability is limited and what is not?

Not well. (a) Yes and (b) Limited liability is having certain assets that cannot be touched by a legal case against my company.

5. What are some aspects or characteristics that many entrepreneurs are focusing too much time on?

Retooling their processes and making more money.

6. What are some aspects or characteristics that many entrepreneurs are either ignoring or spending too little time on?

Creative, excellent work and client relationships, understanding them.

a. Why do you think that these areas are being ignored?

Because making money is easy enough without a lot of consideration. Because we get busy and over commit. Because critical thought is painful.

b. Tell me how this can be changed?

Mentors, co-owners, co-laborers, friends in the industry, all encouraging and giving insight.

7. Tell me about the research you performed before selecting an organizational structure?

I googled "LLC vs Sole Proprietorship"

a. Do you feel you adequately prepared?

No.

b. Tell me more about why you feel you either did or did not?

Because I do not know if I am missing anything legally (even after taking business law in college). It is a complex field.

8. What are some of the aspects or characteristics that you looked at or considered when you created an organizational structure?

How easy. How inexpensive.

9. What, if anything, would you change about your decision on selecting a legal entity if you could?

Not sure. It is just me in my business so far. I would probably have a different answer if I had employees.

Presentation and Discussion of Findings

Data analysis process involves the emergence of themes from the interview transcripts and other collected data, such as the personal journal (Tomkins, 2013). Descriptive coding was used in the coding of the data (Saldana, 2016). In this method, the researcher looks for keywords that highlight the experiences of the interviewee. Tools, such as conditional formatting in Microsoft Word, was used to highlight these keywords if they are present among the other interviews.

Data analysis began by organizing the collected information followed by data perusal, classification, and synthesis (Shenton, 2004). The data analysis approach for exploratory analysis includes (a) compiling the data from the interviews, (b) organizing the data by interviewee, (c) coding of the data (i.e., organizing the data by recognized categories), (d) identifying themes (i.e., the label attached to each recognized category), and (e) establishing data relationships (i.e., recognizing similarities and differences in themes in order to condense or separate themed categories, as appropriate) (Thomas et al., 2015). Once this process was completed, the established themed categories became the findings of the study.

The coding rules that were used to map textual units into data terms was descriptive coding (Saldana, 2016). In descriptive coding, a word or phrase is assigned that summarizes the main topic of a passage (Miles et al., 2014). These codes provide an inventory of topics that highlight the data that was collected.

The technique that was used to translate data terms into themes will be comparing the codes from one data set or interview with others (Saldana, 2016). As similar codes were found in multiple interviews, those would represent commonalities that multiple participants expressed and became themes in the research (Miles et al., 2014).

Theme 1 – Myths and Legends

The first theme that emerged were myths and legends. These are ideas that are taken as fact but not fully understood. In many instances, there is truth at the core, but the idea is not fully understood, and as a result, there are misconceptions about the idea or concept.

Myth 1 – Double Taxation for the C Corporation

Back in the literature review, in the gaps in the literature section, this phenomenon was looked at in detail. Most small businesses do not pay the double taxation, as they take a salary, instead of relying on dividends, which would trigger the double taxation (Raible et al., 2015).

When Participant 1, who is a CPA, was asked about organizational structures, his response was the following.

> I believe pass-through entities are the best organization structure because you avoid double taxation issues C-corporations face.

Myth 2 – Organizing the Business in Another State

This myth is a little more complex, and it does have some truth to it. Roughly half of Fortune 500 companies have incorporated in Delaware, even though they are not physically based there (Lamoreaux, 1998). Delaware has been seen as corporate friendly for some time. There are a few reasons, such as no corporate income tax, special courts for businesses, greater privacy, among other issues. Other states, such as Nevada have enacted similar laws in an attempt to attract businesses to form in their state.

What many small businesses fail to realize, and where the myth comes in, is that they still need to register in their state of operation. For Participant 2, who is physically based on Oklahoma, but organized in Nevada, he will need to pay tax in Oklahoma on the earnings of the business, and they will need to file yearly paperwork for both Oklahoma and Nevada. Most of the benefits of organizing in Delaware and Nevada apply to larger companies, who are looking for venture capital, for instance. For the small business owner, organizing in one state and operating in another will usually result in the added benefit of more paperwork and costs.

Theme 2 – Limited Liability Misunderstood

Limited Liability was another issue that was looked at in depth in the literature review, in the gaps in the literature section. When a business has limited liability as part of its organizational structure, the owners are not held personally liable for the debts and actions of the company (Johnson, 2015).

Participant 1, who is a CPA replied on limited liability.

> I do not believe most entrepreneurs understand legal liability without proper legal assistance. It also limits shareholder liability for claims by creditors against personal assets in the event of default by limiting such claims to the assets of the business.

Participant 3 had similar thoughts on organizing as an LLC.

> I decided to open an LLC because it was my understanding that that would protect my personal assets if things were to go poorly with my practice.

Participant 4 also had similar thoughts.

> I set up an LLC for liability purposes. I wanted my personal assets unaffected in the event of a lawsuit by a client.

Participant 6 offered the following on his understanding.

> When I started my company, I understood I was liable for every aspect of the business. What I did not understand is the degree that would impact my life.

The issue is that many small businesses have an owner that is active in running the business. This opens them up to liability issues that would not be covered under the limited liability that is offered through the organizational structure (Misenti, 2016).

When asked about how entrepreneurs could be protected in this area, Participant 1 replied:

> I think having proper insurance is essential to reducing liability. I believe it is best summed up in the phrase "you don't know what you need, until you need it." The average entrepreneur is not likely to know the areas his/her business will be at risk for legal liability, so they should do their due diligence to seek out legal counsel that specializes in this area and ensures they have the right amount of insurance.

Participant 6 offered the following on insurance and liability.

The purpose of insurance is to shift the financial liability; it does not shift liability in the event of an illegal act on the part of the business officers. Limiting liability allows for the personal assets of the officers to be free from certain seizers by those with legal suits against the corporation.

Participant 7 offered the following on their experience as a web-based business.

In my experience as a virtual (internet-based) business, many business owners, even with dozens of contractors, do not think much about limited liability. Again, this is coming from my own experience, but most of the entrepreneurs that I know hardly consider it since they have very few channels through which they are likely to affect an entity in such a way that makes them liable to a law suit.

Theme 3 – Priorities of the Entrepreneur

A third theme that emerged were some priorities for an entrepreneur as they start their business. These were recommended as priorities for the entrepreneur to focus on and think about as they start their journey. Many entrepreneurs focus much of their attention on other areas, and this list represents areas to focus on to ensure a better chance of organizational success.

Priority 1 – Tax Filing Status

One of the key differences among the various organizational entities is how they treat taxes (McMahonn, 2012). One of the first decisions that the entrepreneur will need to work through is how they want to be taxed, and what type of income taxes do they want to pay.

Participant 6 had the following to say.

In considering an organizational structure one should first ask, what could I lose if I choose the wrong structure, the second is what is going to make the business the most profit considering controllable aspects.

Participant 1 offered the following on selecting a tax filing status.

Failure to understand the income tax consequences of operating as a sole proprietorship, pass-through entity (partnership, LLC, S-corporation), or a C-corporation can result in the loss of personal assets by creditors, lengthy and expensive legal proceedings with other stakeholders, or underpayment of tax liabilities.

Participant 7 had an opposing view of taxes from presented experience.

Taxation details that make a very small difference to the bottom line. From the perspective of a small business with 10 contractors and no W-2 employees, I think that trying to choose a structure that optimizes taxation to the final 1% or 2% can be a vain endeavor. For example, in my opinion there is little reason to consider a C-Corp at this stage if it makes very little difference in the final profit, unless rapid growth is expected in the near future.

Priority 2 – Role of the Entrepreneur in the Business

One area that is often overlooked is the role that the entrepreneur will play in the business. If the entrepreneur will be the only one that is active in the business, then this process is straightforward. If there will be additional people in the business, then the entrepreneur needs to properly organize the business.

Participant 1 offered the following.

I believe corporate org charts should be structured and detailed with a clear chain of command in place. With this comes defined roles, a lack of which can result in discontent.

Participant 6 concurred with Participant 1.

Someone must be the final word on what is and is not going to be accomplished; who reports to whom and when.

Participant 3 had this to say about hiring people for defined roles.

I also think it would've been easier to connect with an accountant and insurance biller earlier than I did. I've since hired both, and it has decreased my stress significantly.

Participant 6 offered the following on the role of the entrepreneur.

An understanding that in the beginning, you must have an ability to do all aspects of the business or the resources to hire someone to do them for you. It is noteworthy that this could affect the legal structure, in that possibly no one would be willing to just be an employee for that function and require you to make them a business partner. In that case, a decision would need to be made as to whether to change the approach.

Participant 7 offered some advice on the role of the entrepreneur in their new business venture.

Many entrepreneurs are very detail-oriented and want to understand every nut and bolt of their business and their finances; this is a good quality to have, but it is impossible to plan for every contingency and some things are better left to experts, for example depending on an accountant that you can trust who specializes in their type of business.

Priority 3 – Organizing the New Business

This is another area where much thought should be given. Some businesses will have a very informal structure, while others will be very formal.

Participant 1 indicated the following.

The entrepreneur should consider from a legal standpoint is the Corporate by-laws or another organizing document. Specifically, who will own the shares, voting rights, and governance of the entity.

Participant 6 indicated the following.

What I cannot control are the laws that allow the governing bodies in my State and Country to reach into my profit margin and thereby effect my ability to employ people, help my family and investing giving into my community. By choosing the right legal structure, I can decide how my business will be viewed by those governing bodies,

Priority 4 – Startup Advice

Participant 6 had some advice for early success.

Writing a business plan that will work. Just because a person may know the mechanics of a business plan doesn't mean they have a workable plan. Having it looked over by an account, multiple business owners that you trust, and a lawyer are in my opinion a good investment of your time and finances.

When asked why many entrepreneurs were ignoring this, Participant 6 offered the following.

A number of reasons, one is excitement; wanting to be the first to implement your business idea. In my opinion, the number one reason is pride. We seem to estimate our knowledge as infinite when the reality is, it is finite.

Participant 3 offered the following advice for entrepreneurs.

My advice to future entrepreneurs who aren't business majors would be to do research and meet with others who have similar businesses to learn from their experience.

Participant 7 offered some advice for getting started.

In my experience the most important consideration for a small, growing business is: What will get you off the ground the fastest? Small businesses need an easy way to get off the ground quickly. Unless there is expectation of hiring dozens of salaried employees in the first year or two, or of reporting profit and loss to third parties, a simple LLC does the trick for hitting the ground running

Participant 5 offered the following advice.

If it's something that you really want, you'll take the time to learn how to do it, even if you don't have any experience or knowledge about it. I would say surround yourself with people who believe in what you're doing because from day to day the temptation to give up comes but having people around you who support you help you to keep going after your dreams!

Priority 5 – Thinking About the Future

When most entrepreneurs are starting their business, their focus is on launching the business and thinking about today. One mistake can be not thinking about the future.

Participant 6 said the following regarding the future.

Understanding that there are uncontrollable aspects, the legal structure should be flexible to allow for change yet provide protection at the same time.

Participant 2 started the business in his own name and later converted the business to an LLC. During this conversion, he experienced many problems with changing information, such as insurance from his name to the name of the LLC. One of his regrets was not starting the business as an LLC.

Participant 4 had the opposite issue.

If I could go back, I probably would stay a DBA. An LLC has A LOT of paperwork to keep track of for the IRS.

Participant 7 had similar thoughts when thinking about the future.

It's essential to choose an organizational structure, but instead of belaboring what would be optimal 10 years in the future, I chose the structure that worked immediately and then simply started working on getting business.

Participant 7 recommended reviewing the decision on organizational structure as the business continues to grow.

Many of the entrepreneurs that I know spend too little time considering how their organizational structure affects their profit and loss over time. It is tempting to choose an organizational structure and simply stick with it for several years, but as the business grows, restructuring is very often a good idea in order to optimize income/profit vs. tax. For example, an LLC is great for getting started as a solopreneur who hires contractors, but as revenue grows, a C-Corp becomes more attractive for the tax advantages. Entrepreneurs should consult their accountants regularly not just for routine purposes, but to reconsider their organizational structure on at least a yearly basis.

Participant 3 thought some about the future when setting up the business.

I chose to do an LLC rather than a PLLC for a couple of reasons: (a) I filed my LLC online and wasn't sure how to do that with a PLLC and (b) I thought the LLC rather than the PLLC left me with more options in case I ever wanted to do just consulting rather than clinical therapy.

Another area is thinking about future funding, such as seeking venture capital. While it may not be a priority today, if it is desired in the future to seek venture capital, it is something to think about today when setting up the business.

Summary of Chapter Four

Chapter 4 was a look at the participants of the study, the presentation of the data, data analysis and the prominent themes that emerged from the data that relate to small business creation and strategies that were derived from the experiences of entrepreneurs. Chapter 5 is the concluding chapter in this study and will present an overview of Chapters 1 through 4. Chapter 5 also includes a summary of the findings related to the research question and problem statement. Chapter 5 will also include the conclusion, findings, implications, and recommendations for further study.

CHAPTER FIVE

This qualitative study focused on strategies business managers need to establish an organizational structure appropriate for entrepreneurial business operations. The single overarching research question was, "What are the strategies business managers need to establish an organizational structure appropriate for entrepreneurial business operations?" Chapter 5 is a summary of the findings and conclusions, as related to the research question, and problem statement. Limitations of the study, recommendations, and the conclusion are included in this chapter.

Findings and Conclusions

This entrepreneurial strategy study used an exploratory qualitative design, supporting the research question, through a set of interview questions. Qualitative research was chosen as it was the best methodology to answer the underlying research question. The interview questions, which were used to collect the data, were constructed using an exploratory design. An exploratory design was also used to collect and interpret the data and understand strategies for entrepreneurial business operations.

In 2015, there were approximately 680,000 new business startups, creating 3 million new jobs (Statistics, 2018). Selecting the wrong business entity for an entrepreneur's situation could cause the business to fail, instead of succeeding (Baik et al., 2015). The population for this study was business managers, in the Tulsa, Oklahoma area that have successfully established organizational structures for entrepreneurial business operations. The estimated size of the population is 60,000. This population is appropriate because approximately 12% of adults are starting or in the process of starting a new business, and the adult population of Tulsa County is approximately 490,000 (Kelley et al., 2017).

Eight participants who are entrepreneurs, or advisers, in Tulsa, Oklahoma, shared their knowledge and stories with the researcher. The participants consisted of five males and three females, from a variety of industries and backgrounds. Data was collected by asking the participants 10 open-ended questions. Descriptive coding was used to highlight the key points of the data. The key points merged to become three major themes that could be broken down into subcategories.

Theme 1 – Myths and Legends

Two myths emerged from the data. The first one is the double taxation for the C corporation. Most small businesses do not pay the double taxation, as they take a salary, instead of relying on dividends, which would trigger the double taxation (Raible et al., 2015). After much research, this myth is still prevalent in the literature and was discussed heavily in the gaps in the literature section during the literature review. The unfortunate aspect of this myth is that many entrepreneurs merely ignore this entity and look elsewhere when the C corporation has many unique features that could benefit the entrepreneur if the C corporation was better understood (Calcagni, 2010).

The second myth that emerged is the potential benefits of organizing the business in another state. While there is much truth to this, and approximately half of Fortune 500 companies have incorporated in Delaware, even though they are not physically based there (Lamoreaux, 1998). While there is some benefit for a large company, for the average startup, there is little benefit, and it could cost them. For a company physically located in Oklahoma, and organized in Nevada, they would need to file in both states and likely pay some form of corporate tax in both states.

Theme 2 – Limited Liability Misunderstood

Limited Liability was a second theme that emerged from the data and was another issue that was looked at in depth in the literature review, in the gaps in the literature section. When a business has limited liability as part of its organizational structure, the owners are not held personally liable for the debts and actions of the company (Johnson, 2015). While the participants understood this part of limited liability, what the participants did not understand is the limited liability protects them as an owner, but not as someone who is actively running the business, which is likely the case for most entrepreneurs.

The entrepreneur who is actively running the business will need to be concerned with committing a tort, which opens them up to liability issues that would not be covered under the limited liability that is offered through the organizational structure (Misenti, 2016). Participant 4, who has a home daycare, would be a fitting example of this phenomenon. This participant should be concerned with issues, such as slip and falls and other areas of negligence, while this participant would not be protected under limited liability for those acts since the participant is personally responsible. Many entrepreneurs would likely be better served by focusing on having proper insurance that would personally protect them, instead of focusing on limited liability that would only protect them as an owner.

Theme 3 – Priorities of the Entrepreneur

A third theme that emerged were priorities for the entrepreneur as they start their new business ventures. These priorities represent advice that the participants would give to fellow entrepreneurs. The participants shared many things that they would either change, or that worked for them and wanted to pass these on to future entrepreneurs.

Priority 1 – Tax Filing Status

One of the critical differences among the various organizational entities is how they treat taxes (McMahonn, 2012). Most of the entities have pass-through taxation, where the profits from the business flow through to the entrepreneur's personal income taxes. Many entrepreneurs fail to realize that they will need to pay taxes on the full profit of the business, and not just on the profits that the entrepreneur brings home. This phenomenon will cause many startup businesses, who want to keep money in the business, to only take enough out in order to pay the taxes.

The C corporation is the one exception to the pass-through taxation, though some entities, such as the LLC can elect corporate taxation status. In the corporate taxation method, the company would pay corporate tax rates on the profits, and the remaining profit would be retained for future use. Any profits that the owners elected to withdraw could be made so in the form of dividends.

Priority 2 – Role of the Entrepreneur in the Business

Another priority for the entrepreneur is the role that the entrepreneur should have in the new business venture, while this is not an issue for an entrepreneur that is the sole worker in the business (Winrow, 2008). It becomes an issue as the business grows and employees are hired. Many entrepreneurs will have a challenging time with letting go of handling every aspect of the business and let others handle aspects of the business. The one piece of consistent advice was to have well-defined roles for everyone in the business, including the use of organization charts, to define who each person in the organization reports to clearly.

Priority 3 – Organizing the New Business

Another priority, and one that is often overlooked is organizing the new business. One of the priorities here is deciding on the governance of the new venture (Sumutka, 1997). A corporate structure will have shareholders, who will elect a board. The board will elect officers to run the business. For many small corporations, the entrepreneurs will handle all of these roles. If the entrepreneurs elect an LLC, they can run the LLC, or they can hire a manager to handle the day to day operations. If there are multiple entrepreneurs, this process will also include how voting rights will be handled, with each person receiving equal votes, or will the voting share be based on the percent of capital that each entrepreneur contributed?

Priority 4 – Startup Advice

The previous priorities were to help the entrepreneur set up the framework for the new business (Baik et al., 2015). This priority is geared towards steps to take as the business is ready to launch. One of the recommendations that were common for many of the participants was to have a well-written business plan, and to have the plan looked at by legal and financial professionals as well as other business owners.

Many entrepreneurs do not have a business background, and this was the case for many of the participants in this study. Some of the participants got around this by researching the areas where they were lacking, as well as learning from people who have a similar business, to see how they handled these deficiencies. Other participants suggested taking the time to learn about the areas where the entrepreneur was deficient.

Priority 5 – Thinking About the Future

The final priority is to think about the future, even as the business is just getting started (Hertz et al., 2009). Many entrepreneurs will start a business with one type of entity and later convert to another as the business grows and the needs of the entrepreneur change. This priority is one area where there was some disagreement with the participants. One participant wished they had converted at the beginning, while another wished they had never converted, as it meant more paperwork. Another participant suggested to find the best entity for today, and not worry about the future, while another participant suggested reviewing the organizational structure regularly, to make sure it is what is best for the business. One of the participants, who is a counselor, could have elected an entity for medical professionals, but chose a standard LLC, in the event the participant did not want to counsel people but wanted to do consulting work as well.

Limitations of the Study

The researcher devised 10 distinct interview questions to explore the strategies of entrepreneurs in Tulsa, Oklahoma, to understand strategies for creating an entrepreneurial organizational structure. The researcher understood that there are limitations and areas still exist for future research. The model that developed as a conceptual framework for creating strategies for entrepreneurial business operations is invigorating, however, there are some weaknesses to the study.

This research started with three limitations. The first limitation of this research was the honesty of the responses of the participants. A second limitation on this study was the time available for this study. A third limitation was the reliability and validity of the questions that were asked.

After completing the research, a few discrete limitations were evident. The first limitation is methodology. This research design leveraged a qualitative approach to develop the research question. The possibility remains, however, that this methodology was not the best approach to answer the research question. All the possible variables that lead to the strategies of entrepreneurial organizational success were not ascertained by the research design. As an example, the research design did not consider legal aspects of organizational success, as entrepreneurs were interviewed, and not business law attorneys. The sample size could have also been more substantial, added more advisory personnel, and included a more diverse background of participants. The geographic boundary could have been expanded, which could have netted more details that could have influenced the results. Finally, there is the possibility of coding errors, which could be the result of the researcher choosing the wrong descriptive words during the coding process.

Implications for Practice

This research focused on the strategies business managers need to establish an organizational structure appropriate for entrepreneurial business operations. During the research, it became apparent that there were areas where gaps existed that represented areas where improvements could be made that could benefit future entrepreneurs. Two of these areas will be looked at and discussed.

Area 1 – Business Education for Non-Business Backgrounds

Many people are under the assumption that all entrepreneurs have a background in business, or they should have that knowledge before becoming entrepreneurs (Blair & Marcum, 2015). This was an area where the literature was either silent or assumed entrepreneurs would seek professional assistance in areas where they were deficient in knowledge. Having that background, people feel, would give the entrepreneur the tools that they need to become successful. The reality is that many entrepreneurs do not have any formal training in business, but instead have training in their area of expertise. This was the case for 4 of the 8 participants in this study. Two of the participants have advanced degrees in counseling, and are knowledgeable in helping others, but did not receive any training in business before beginning their entrepreneurial journey.

One area where an educational opportunity exists would be in formal education. A class could be developed as an elective for non-business majors where they could receive an overview of the various business disciplines, as well as an overview of business law. While not a thorough education, it would give the potential entrepreneurs at least a working knowledge of varied topics, and a knowledge of what to look for when hiring either staff or outside professionals to handle various areas, such as accounting. This type of educational opportunity would be very ---- beneficial to the community college, where many receive an applied associate in a field, and then begin to work in that field.

Outside of formal education, this type of education could be offered within the community and could be hosted at community centers, churches, or other areas with free space. It could be offered one night a week for several weeks. Each week would be a different topic, and the class would be led by a professional in that field, who would volunteer their time. As an example, the first week could be on business law. A local attorney would volunteer to lead that class and give a background on business law, including business formation, contracts, and handling legal disputes. This type of learning environment would be beneficial to both the potential entrepreneur, as well as the established entrepreneur, who would like more information on a topic.

Area 2 – Business Entity Research

Going into this study, one of the areas where the researcher wanted more information, was on where entrepreneurs were going to do their research on selecting the best organizational structure for their new venture. There are a variety of sources from books to websites to professionals that specialize in this area. Where the entreprneur went to seek information on selecting their organizational structure was ones of the questions that all of the participants were asked, and the results are below in Table 2.

Table 2

Sources of Research

Participant	Major source of research for their organizational structure
1	N/A. Participant is advisor, and not entrepreneur.
2	Business partner from another business venture
3	Oklahoma Commerce Department and Secretary of State website
4	Husband, who spoke to business people
5	Facebook groups, Instagram, podcasts, and YouTube
6	Chose not to answer
7	Business mentors and online searches
8	Google search

As the table demonstrates, at least for the sample that was chosen, entrepreneurs, for the most part, are doing informal searches for relevant information on organizational structures. The issue with using an informal search is that the information being presented is questionable and is not being tailored to the needs of the entrepreneur (Hopson & Hopson, 2014). One of the more popular options for the entrepreneur are websites, such as LegalZoom that do offer some information, and are popular for their ability to ask a few questions of the entrepreneur and within minutes have the appropriate organizational paperwork filled out and ready to be filed with the state. The issue with them is that the information is not customizable to the entrepreneur and their needs. They are best for the entrepreneur who has a great understanding of organizational structures and is merely looking for a way to file the paperwork with the state.

No one in the above table mentioned a business law attorney, accountant, or another professional for the primary source of research. Are entrepreneurs not seeking legal advice, because they consider their business too small to warrant professional legal advice or is the pricing vague or perceived to be too high for their needs? The lack of entrepreneurs seeking professional advice is another area where there is an opportunity for better education and transparency from the professional community. An opportunity exists for professionals to offer educational opportunities where they volunteer to speak to the community or entrepreneurship and selecting an organizational structure. As part of attending the seminar, the attorney could offer packages where the organizational paperwork will be filed with the appropriate state agency and X number of hours of legal advice could be included for a set price.

Implications of Study and Recommendations for Future Research

This qualitative study was designed to understand the strategies business managers need to establish an organizational structure appropriate for entrepreneurial business operations by reviewing the literature and interviewing study participants. Study participants provided abundant data that described their strategies that lead to creating their organizational structure. The findings and issues that were raised by the current study signify several possible opportunities for future research.

Opportunity 1 – Seeking Professional Advice

One opportunity for future research could use many of the same questions but instead focus on asking them to professionals, such as business law attorneys and accountants (Hertz et al., 2009). These professionals advise entrepreneurs and their input could add more depth, as they actively involved in the field of entrepreneurship. While the average entrepreneur is in startup mode for a few months or years, these professionals are in this mode for most of their career. The researcher initially wanted to interview some for this study, but it was easier to find entrepreneurs who were willing to participate, and interviewing the entrepreneurs was a good foundation, on which future research could be built upon.

Opportunity 2 – A Longitudinal Study

This second opportunity lies outside of the realm of possibility for a doctoral program, but it is within reach of one who is wanting to study this field over the long term (Hertz et al., 2009). The researcher could follow one or two entrepreneurs, as they start their entrepreneurial journey. Every so often the researcher could check in with the entrepreneurs to not only see how they have progressed but also how the entrepreneurs feel about the choices they have made. As an example, two of the participants of this study expressed frustration over the timing of their choice to convert to an LLC. It can take an entrepreneur some time to fully understand their selection of an organizational structure. Some paperwork and taxes will only be handled once a year, while some corporate structures have yearly board and shareholder meetings. It may take doing these yearly functions more than once to fully grasp the totality of the situation and understand the choices that were made.

Opportunity 3 – Seeking Experienced Business Operators

A third opportunity would be to ask these same types of questions, but to ask them of business operators, who have been operating their business for some time, say 10 years, and were also the founder of the particular business (Treusch, 2003). This length of time would allow the business operator to adequately reflect on decisions that were made at the beginning and things that could be done differently. It is possible to find that too much time was spent on an aspect of the business that turned out to be not as important as first thought. The insight of these experienced managers could give new entrepreneurs a better idea of what is essential to focus on, and some things that should receive less focus.

Reflections

The idea for this study started while reading some books, for the local library's summer reading program, on small business creation three summers ago. Countless hours have been spent researching this topic, from a variety of sources. Many Saturday afternoons have been spent writing and editing this research paper when the researcher would instead be doing other things. Along the way though, the researcher not only has learned how to be a better writer but has gone from a consumer of data and thoughts, but to an academic creator of thoughts and data for others to consume and analyze. While this journey has been difficult, and the researcher had doubts that the journey would be completed, this experience has been a journey worth undertaking, and the researcher is better off for having completed it.

Conclusion

This study was designed to examine the strategies business managers need to establish an organizational structure appropriate for entrepreneurial business operations, by exploring the experiences of entrepreneurs in the Tulsa, Oklahoma area to see what strategies they used when creating their own entrepreneurial organizational structure. These strategies were analyzed to create some answers to the research question, "What are the strategies business managers need to establish an organizational structure appropriate for entrepreneurial business operations?"

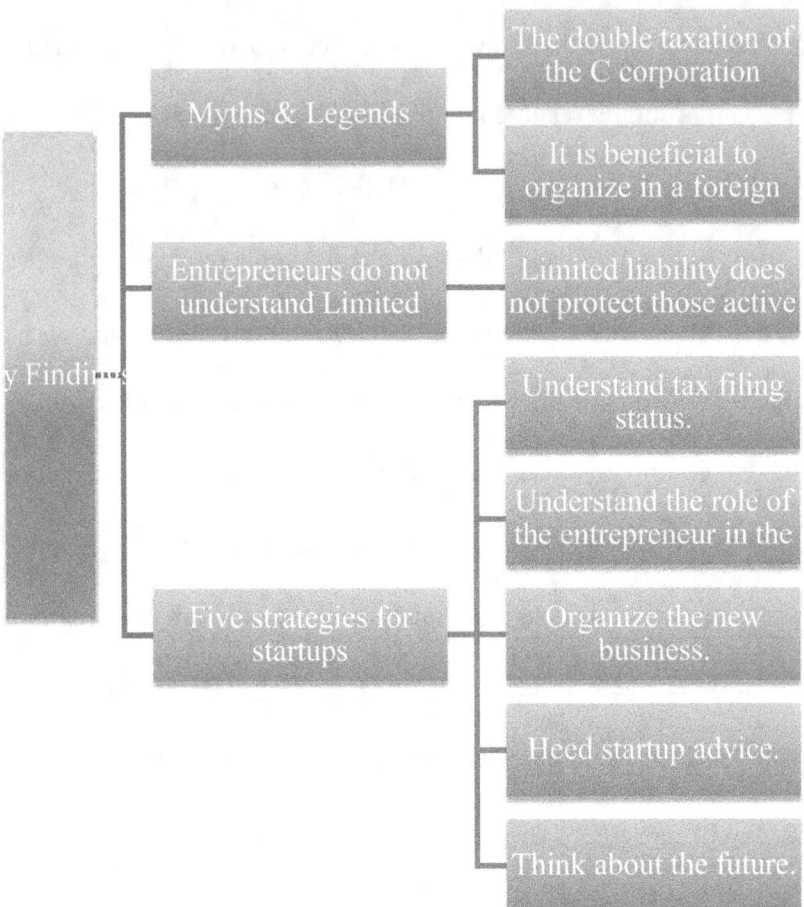

Figure 2 Key Findings

Critical attributes of creating an organizational structure were identified and analyzed. The key findings highlighted two areas where there is much misunderstanding in the entrepreneurial community, the first of which is that entrepreneurs should avoid the C corporation, as it has double taxation. While this can be the case, most small businesses do not pay it, and instead distribute money to the owners via salaries, as opposed to dividends, which would trigger the double taxation. The second misunderstanding is that it can be beneficial to organize the business in another state. While there may be some benefits, for small businesses the extra costs and work will outweigh the benefits.

A second key finding is the misunderstanding most entrepreneurs have with regards to limited liability that is provided as part of many organizational structures. What many entrepreneurs fail to realize is that the limited liability protects them as an owner of the business, and not as an active participant in the business. Failing to understand the difference can leave the entrepreneur vulnerable to lawsuits, which could cause the business to fail and leave their personal assets at risk.

The final key finding were five strategies to assist entrepreneurs in setting up their new business venture. The five strategies are to understand tax filing status, the role of the entrepreneur in the business, organize the new business, heed startup advice, and think about the future. These five strategies give the entrepreneur areas to focus on as they are starting their entrepreneurial journey.

There are a few implications that arise from these findings. The first one is the need for entrepreneurs to seek professional assistance as they are starting their entrepreneurial journey. Too often they rely solely on the internet for their research. While many entrepreneurs may not be able to afford an attorney for every aspect of setting up their business, it would not be out outside of the realm of possibility to sit down for an hour or two to go over some of the key decisions. The same principal applies to spending time to understand the tax differences among the different organizational structures, and how it would impact their household taxes. Entrepreneurs should also seek assistance from business insurance providers. This is one of the areas in which entrepreneurs often leave themselves vulnerable.

A second implication that arises from the findings is the need for education for entrepreneurs. Entrepreneurs know the business that they are involved in, but there are many areas where they need support. As mentioned in the last section, they often do not understand legal, accounting, and insurance issues. Many entrepreneurs do not have a business background, and they would benefit from understanding basic business principals, such as writing a business plan, hiring employees, and handling basic bookkeeping tasks. A case has already been made for formal and informal ways of providing education to entrepreneurs. This educational issue could also be provided by experienced business leaders who could provide mentoring, which would allow the entrepreneurs to benefit from the experience of the business mentor.

A final implication that arises from the findings is the need to encourage entrepreneurship. Often in society people will think they need an MBA and/ or a large sum of money before they can start a business. The educational workshops that were mentioned earlier could also have a focus on those that are interested in having their own business, but they are unsure of where to start or what steps they would need to undertake in order to begin their own entrepreneurial journey.

REFERENCES

Alberty, S. C. (2003). The S Corporation: Your Best Choice For An Established Small Business. *Practical Lawyer* (December), p11-19.

Altieri, M. P., & Cenker, W. J. (2002). Partnerships, LLCs, LLPs, and S Corporations. *CPA Journal, 72* (October), p40-47.

Anderson, B. (2004). Benefit Issues Regarding Partnerships, S Corporations, and Sole Proprietorships. *Journal of Pension Benefits: Issues in Administration*, p26-31.

Andre, R. (2012). Assessing the Accountability of the Benefit Corporation: Will This New Gray Sector Organization Enhance Corporate Social Responsibility? *Journal of Business Ethics* (March), p133-150.

Artz, N., & Sutherland, J. (2010). Low-Profit Limited Liability Companies (L3Cs): Competitiveness Implications. *Competition Forum, 8*, p279-286.

Bahena, A. J. (2010). Series LLCs: The Asset Protection Dream Machines? *The Journal of Corporation Law, 35* (4), p799-825.

Baik, Y., Lee, S., & Lee, C. (2015). Entrepreneurial firms' choice of ownership forms. *International Entrepreneurship and Management Journal* (November), p453-471.

Banoff, S. I., & Lipton, R. M. (2003). Revisiting what's more popular: Partnerships, LLCs, or S Corporations? *Journal of Taxation, 99* (September), p189-190.

Blair, E. S., & Marcum, T. M. (2015). Heed Our Advice: Exploring How Professionals Guide Small Business Owners in Start-Up Entity Choice. *Journal of Small Business Management, 53*, p249–265.

Blair, E. S., Marcum, T. M., & Fry, F. F. (2009). The Disproportionate Costs Of Forming LLCs Vs. Corporations: The Impact On Small Firm Liability Protection. *Journal of Small Business Strategy, 20* (Fall/ Winter), p23-41.

Burton, H., & Karlinsky, S. S. (2007). Current Developments in S Corporations (Part II). *Tax Adviser* (November), p786-795.

Calcagni, D. (2010). Revisiting an Old Friend: Financial Planning for C Corporation Employee-Shareholders. *Journal of Financial Service Professionals* (March), p6-13.

Campbell, T. H. (1994). When is it appropriate to use a limited liability company? *Journal of Financial Planning* (January), p25-32.

Chrisman, R. D. (2010). LLC'S are the New King of the Hill. *Fordham Journal of Corporate & Financial Law*, p459-489.

Cleveland, G. A., Wells, W. R., & Yoshimoto, G. A. (1996). Is There a Limited Liability Company in your Future? *Review of Business, 17* (Spring), p26-31.

Collins, J. M., & Bey, R. P. (1986). The Master Limited Partnership:An Alternative to the Corporation. *Financial Management* (Winter), p5-14.

Converse, M. (2012). Philosophy of phenomenology: how understanding aids research. *Nurse Researcher*, p28-32.

Creswell, J. (1998). *Qualitative inquiry and research design: Choosing among five traditions.* Thousand Oaks: Sage.

Cruz, C. A., & Karayan, J. E. (1996). Should your firm operate as a LLC? *Business Forum, 21* (Summer/ Fall), p16-21.

Donohoe, M. P., Lisowsky, P., & Mayberry, M. A. (2015). Who Benefits From the Tax Advantages Of Organizational Form Choice? *National Tax Journal, 68* (December), p975-997.

Ellentuck, A. (2010). Converting a C Corporation Into an LLC. *The Tax Adviser* (June), p426-427.

Estabrook, T. J. (2009). Factors To Consider When Making A Choice-Of-Entity Decision. *Practical Tax Strategies, 83* (August), p68-78.

Evans, J. N., & Castilla, M. L. (2013). Despite Higher Tax Rates, S Corporations Retain Advantages Over C Corporations. *Practical Tax Strategies* (December), p271-273.

Everett, J. O., Raabe, W. A., & Hennig, C. J. (2011). Planning Considerations When Converting a C Corporation to an LLC. *Tax Adviser, 42* (February), p110-111.

Eyal-Cohen, M. (2009). The Past, Present, and Future of Small Business Tax Preferences. In: (Doctoral Dissertation).

Fellows, J. A., & Jewell, J. F. (2007). S Corporation Profits or Payday? *Journal of Accountancy, 204* (September), p60-63.

Geekie, J. T., & McClain, B. w. (2014). Legal and Tax Considerations in Choosing the Form of Business Under U.S. Laws. *International Journal of Arts & Sciences, 7* (1), p33-43.

Geisler, G. G., & Wallace, S. (2005). The Use of Compensation for Tax Avoidance by Owners of Small Corporations. *The Journal of the American Taxation Association, 27* (Spring), p73-90,105.

Gesiko, A. (2008). Structure Counts! The Tax Implications Arising From the Formation, Operation and Liquidation of C Corporations, S orporations, Partnerships and Limited Liability Companies. *Corporate Business Taxation Monthly* (November), p39-50.

Gilbert, S. (2008). On the Difficulties of Taxing Disregarded Single Member Limited Liability Companies as Corporations for Employment Taxes. *The Tax Lawyer* (Spring), p969-980.

Gomtsian, S. (2015). The Governance Of Publicly Traded Limited Liability Companies. *Delaware Journal of Corporate Law, 40*, p207-279.

Guenther, D. A. (1990). The Effect of Income Taxes on the Form of Business Entity. In: (Doctoral Dissertation).

Hansmann, H., Kraakman, R., & Squire, R. (2007). The New Business Entities in Evolutionary Perspective. *European Business Organization Law Review* (8), p59-69.

Hennink, M., Hutter, I., & Bailey, A. (2011). *Qualitative Research Methods*. Thousand Oaks: SAGE Publiccations, Inc.

Henzler, J., & Milani, K. (2014). The Master Limited Partnership: A Hybrid Structure for Natural Resource Firms. *Taxes* (April), p53-58,68.

Hertz, G. T., Beasley, F., & White, R. J. (2009). Selecting A Legal Structure: Revisiting The Strategic Issues And Views Of Small And Micro Business Owners. *Journal of Small Business Strategy, 20* (Spring/ Summer), p81-101.

Hiller, J. (2013). The Benefit Corporation and Corporate Social Responsibility. *Journal of Business Ethics* (118), p287-301.

Hodder, L., McAnally, M. L., & Weaver, C. D. (2003). The Influence of Tax and Nontax Factors on Banks' Choice of Organizational Form. *Accounting Review, 78* (January), p297-325.

Hopson, J., & Hopson, P. (2014). Making the Right Choice of Business Entity. *The CPA Journal* (October), p42-47.

Jenkins, G. E. (1988). The Impact of Choice of Entity Selection Upon Compensation. *Journal of the American Society of CLU & ChFC, 42* (March), p30-39.

Johnson, L. R. (2015). From GP To LLC Making the Right Choice of Entity Decision. *Journal of the International Academy for Case Studies, 21* (November), p159-167.

Jurinski, J. J. (2004). Family Limited Partnerships: A Primer on the Risks and Rewards. *Journal of Financial Service Professionals, 58* (May), p46-55.

Karl, P. (1999). The answers point to the LLC: Twenty questions on selections of a legal entity. *The CPA Journal* (August), p40-45.

Karlinsky, S. S., & Burton, H. (2008). Current Developments in S Corporations (Part I). *The Tax Adviser* (October), p678-686.

Kelley, D., Ali, A., Brush, C., Corbett, A., Kim, P., & Majbouri, M. (2017). *Global Entrepreneurship Monitor United States Report 2016*. Retrieved from Babson Park:

Khandekar, R. P., & Young, J. E. (1985). Selecting A Legal Structure A Strategic Decision. *Journal of Small Business Management* (January), p47-55.

Lamoreaux, N. R. (1998). Partnerships, Corporations, and the Theory of the Firm. *American Rconomic Review, 88*, p66-71.

Land, S. B. (2009). Entity Identity: The Taxation of Quasi-Separate Enterprises. *The Tax Lawyer* (Fall), p99-167.

Langemeier, B. L. (1987). A Model of Choice of Business Entity Using Discriminate Analysis. In: (Doctoral Dissertation).

Leimberg, S. R. (1994). The financial services professional's guide to limited liability companies (LLCs). *Journal of the American Society of CLU & ChFC, 48* (November), p48.

Luna, L., & Murray, M. N. (2010). The Effects of State Tax Structure on Business Organizational Form. *National Tax Journal, 63* (December), p995-1021.

Lynch, M. F., Casten, D. B., & Beausejour, D. (2012). Now Is the Time: Converting a C Corporation to an S Corporation or LLC. *Tax Adviser*, p534-542.

McMahon, M. J., & Simmons, D. L. (2014). When Subchapter S Meets Subchapter C. *Tax Lawyer, 67* (2), p231-309.

McMahonn, M. J., JR. (2012). Now You See It, Now You Don't: The Comings and Goings of Disregarded Entities. *The Tax Lawyer* (Winter), p259-307.

McNulty, M. A., & Kwon, M. M. (2006). Tax Considerations in Choice of Entity Decision. *Business Entities, 8* (May/ June), p28-43.

Miles, M., Huberman, M., & Saldana, J. (2014). *Qualitative Data Analysis: A Methods Sourcebook*. Thousand Oaks: Sage.

Miller, S. K. (2014). The Best of Both Worlds: Default Fiduciary Duties and Contractual Freedom in Alternative Business Entities. *Journal of Corporation Law, 39* (2), p295-345.

Misenti, N. C. (2016). Personal Liability For Commission of a Tort: A Significant, and Often Overlooked, Exception to Limited Liability In The LLC and Corporation. *Southern Journal of Business and Ethics, 8*, p11-37.

Nevius, A. (2007). Disregarded Entities Held in High Regard. *Journal of Accountancy, 204* (August), p78.

Nevius, A. (2010). Series LLCs: Pros and Cons of a Growing Trend. *Journal of Accountancy, 209* (January), p64.

Nithman, R. W. (2015). Business Entity Selection: Why It Matters to Healthcare Practitioners Part I–Conceptual Framework, Sole Proprietorships, and Partnerships. *The Journal of Medical Practice Management*, p358-361.

Nithman, R. W. (2016). Business Entity Selection: Why It Matters to Healthcare Practitioners Part II—Corporations, Limited Liability Companies, and Professional Entities. *Practice Management*, p377-380.

Nithman, R. W. (2017). Business Entity Selection: Why It Matters to Healthcare Practitioners Part III—Nonprofits, Ethics, Practice Implications, and Conclusions. *The Journal of Medical Practice Management*, p36-39.

Openshaw, N. (2002). LLPs: Possible Benefits, Potential Limitations. *In Practice* (July/ August), p407-409.

Opiela, N. (2004). According to Form: Choosing the Right Business Entity. *Journal of Financial Planning* (July), p36-42.

Ostrov, J. (2000). Single member LLC's and other disregarded entities. *Tax Management Estates, Gifts and Trusts Journal, 25* (November), p284-297.

Petravick, G., & Troutman, C. (2007). Has the LLC Replaced the S Corporation As the Entrepreneur's Entity Choice? *Business Entities* (November/ December), p18-27.

Raible, D. G., Teti, R., & Brinker, T. M. (2015). Is the C Corporation a Better Business Form Than the S Corporation for Today's Entrepreneurs? *Journal of Financial Service Professionals* (May), p14-17.

Riles, J., & Whitlock, B. (2003). The ABCs of LLCs. *The National Public Accountant* (September), p35-36.

Rothman, R. P. (2007). Translating Corporate Concepts into the Language of LLCs. *The Tax Lawyer* (Fall), p163-240.

Rubin, H. J., & Rubin, I. (2005). *Qualitative interviewing: the art of hearing data*. London: Sage Publications.

Saldana, J. (2016). *The Coding Manual for Qualitative Researchers*. Los Angeles: Sage.

Samson, W. D., & McLeod, R. W. (1990). Choosing Between C Versus S Corporate Status. *Journal of the American Society of CLU & ChFC* (September), p62-75.

Schatz, L. B., Gorski, W. J., & Schatz, N. (1996). What every insurance professional needs to know about limited liability companies. *Journal of Financial Service Professionals, 50* (May), p80.

Schnee, E. J. (2006). Advances To S Corporations. *Journal of Accountancy* (March), 77.

Schwidetzky, W. D. (2009). Integrating Subchapters K and S-Just Do It. *The Tax Lawyer* (Spring), p749-821.

Sellers, K., & Tripp, J. C. (2015). Converting from C to S corp. may be costlier than you think. *Journal of Accountancy;*, p64-69.

Shanney-Saborsky, R. (1998). S-corps and ESOPs: Too early to tell? *Journal of Financial Planning, 11* (February), p28-30.

Shenton, A. (2004). Strategies for ensuring trustworthiness in qualitative. *Education for Information*, p63-75.

Sicular, D. (2014). Subchapter S at 55-Has Time Passed This Passthrough By? Maybe Not. *Tax Lawyer* (Fall), p185-238.

Stancil, J. L. (2012). Has the S Corporation Outlived Its Usefulness? *The CPA Journal* (February), p40-45.

Statistics, U. S. B. o. L. (Producer). (2018, August 23). Entrepreneurship and the U.S. Economy. *U.S. Bureau of Labor Statistics*. Retrieved from https://www.bls.gov/bdm/entrepreneurship/entrepreneurship.htm

Summa, J. D. (1996). Should you convert to a limited liability company? . *Journal of the American Society of CLU & ChFC, 66* (April), p57-62.

Sumutka, A. (1997). Selecting a Form of Business. *CPA Journal, 66* (April), p24-29.

Thomas, J., Nelson, J., & Silverman, S. (2015). *Research Methods in Physical Activity-7th Edition*. Champaign: Human Kinetics.

Tomkins, L., & Eatough, V. (2013). The feel of experience: Phenomenological ideas for organizational research. *Qualitative Research in Organizations and Management: An International Journal*, p258-275.

Tracy, S. (2013). *Qualitative Research Methods: Collecting Evidence, Crafting Analysis, Communicating Impact*. West Sussex: Blackwell.

Treusch, P. E. (2003). Advising a client on the best form in which to conduct a business. *The Practical Tax Lawyer* (Fall), p35-52.

Vaughan, S. K., & Arsneault, S. (2018). The Public Benefit of Benefit Corporations. *PS, Political Science & Politics* (January), p54-60.

Wells, W. (1994). Limited liability companies: Something new, something different. *Journal of Small Business Management, 32* (January), p78-82.

Wells, W., & Yoshimoto, G. (1993). The Limited Liability Company: An Analysis. *Mid - American Journal of Business*, p37-44.

Winrow, B. P. (2008). Transformation of the Viable Business Structures. *The Entrepreneurial Executive, 13*, p63-81.

APPENDIX A

Informed Consent

Title of Study: THE STRATEGIES BUSINESS MANAGERS NEED TO ESTABLISH AN ORGANIZATIONAL STRUCTURE APPROPRIATE FOR ENTREPRENEURIAL BUSINESS OPERATIONS.

Investigator: Kevin DeVault

Contact Number: XXX-XXX-XXXX

Purpose of the Study

You are invited to participate in a research study. The purpose of this study is to explore the strategies business managers need to establish an organizational structure appropriate for entrepreneurial business operation.

Participants

You are being asked to participate in the study because your opinions, outlook, and insights concerning the research question are critical to understanding this phenomenon.

Procedures

If you volunteer to participate in this study, you will be asked to do the following: participate in a one on one interview to discuss your thought and opinions on business organizational structure.

Benefits of Participation

There may/may not be direct benefits to you as a participant in this study. However, we hope to learn strategies to assist entrepreneurs when they select an organizational structure.

Risks of Participation

There are risks involved in all research studies. This study is estimated to involve minimal risk. An example of this risk is possibly feeling uncomfortable answering questions about your organization or your clients.

Cost/Compensation

This will be no financial cost to you to participate in this study. The study will take 30-60 minutes. You will not be compensated for your time. *Colorado Technical University will not provide compensation or free medical care for an unanticipated injury sustained as a result of participating in this research study.*

Contact Information

If you have any questions or concerns about the study, you may contact Kevin DeVault <u>and</u> mentor Dr. Daniel Dayton, XXXXXX@coloradotech.edu, and XXX-XXX-XXXX). For questions regarding the rights of research subjects, any complaints or comments regarding the manner in which the study is being conducted, you may contact Colorado Technical University – Doctoral Programs at 719-598-0200.

Voluntary Participation

Your participation in this study is voluntary. You may refuse to participate in this study or in any part of this study. You may withdraw at any time without prejudice. You are encouraged to ask questions about this study at the beginning or at any time during the research study.

Confidentiality

All data will remain confidential, and will be stored in encrypted files, and stored in a secure environment.

Participant Consent

I have read the above information and agree to participate in this study. I am at least 18 years of age. A copy of this form has been given to me.

_____   _____

Signature of ParticipantDate

_____

Participant Name (Please Print)

APPENDIX B

Interview Questions

List all of the interview questions here.

1. One of the strategies in establishing an organizational structure is understanding the needs of the entrepreneur in terms of what an organizational structure can provide. Can you describe the factors or characteristics that an entrepreneur should consider when selecting a legal organizational structure?
2. What are the most significant characteristics to consider when deciding on an organizational structure?
3. What are the least significant characteristics to consider?
4. One aspect that attracts people to forming an organization structure is limited liability. How well do you think entrepreneurs understand what liability is limited and what is not?
5. What are some aspects or characteristics that many entrepreneurs are focusing too much time on?
6. What are some aspects or characteristics that many entrepreneurs are either ignoring or spending too little time on?
7. Tell me about the research you performed before selecting an organizational structure?
8. What are some of the aspects or characteristics that you looked at or considered when you created an organizational structure?
9. What, if anything, would you change about your decision on selecting a legal entity if you could?
10. What other items should be added to our discussion?

APPENDIX C

Interview Protocol

1. Explain the purpose of the study.

2. Assure participant confidentiality and have the participant sign the informed consent agreement form.

3. Address participant physical comfort concerns (lighting, room temperature, chair, and ambient noise distraction, make water available.

4. Record the subject's number on the top of the interview field notes.

5. Encourage participants to open up about their experiences.

6. Monitor participant body language to minimize influencing subject answers.

7. Precisely record participant responses and annotate any non-verbal responses.

8. Audio record and assign a chronological number to each interview.

9. Ask interview questions in order and ask follow-on questions for clarification (see Appendix C).

Interview and follow-on questions:

1. One of the strategies in establishing an organizational structure is understanding the needs of the entrepreneur in terms of what an organizational structure can provide. Can you describe the factors or characteristics that an entrepreneur should consider when selecting a legal organizational structure?

Follow-on question 1: Tell me more about why these should be considered.

Follow-on question 2: Did I understand you correctly when you said (repeat participant response).

2. What are the most significant characteristics to consider when deciding on an organizational structure?

> Follow-on question 1: Did I understand you correctly when you said (repeat participant response)
>> Follow-on question 2: Tell me more about why these are the most important to consider.

3. What are the least significant characteristics to consider?

> Follow-on question 1: Did I understand you correctly when you said (repeat participant response)
>> Follow-on question 2: Tell me more about why these are the least important to consider.

4. One aspect that attracts people to forming an organization structure is limited liability. How well do you think entrepreneurs understand what liability is limited and what is not?

> Follow-on question 1: Do you think that having proper insurance would help in reducing liability?
> Follow-on question 2: For clarification, will you elaborate on limited liability?

5. What are some aspects or characteristics that many entrepreneurs are focusing too much time on?

> Follow-on question 1: Why do you think that entrepreneurs are focusing so much on these?
> Follow-on question 2: Tel lme how this can be changed?

6. What are some aspects or characteristics that many entrepreneurs are either ignoring or spending too little time on?

Follow-on question 1: Why do you think that these areas are being ignored?

Follow-on question 2: Tell me how this can be changed?

7. Tell me about the research you performed before selecting an organizational structure?

Follow-on question 1: Do you feel you adequately prepared?

Follow-on question 2: Tell me more about why you feel you either did or did not?

8. What are some of the aspects or characteristics that you looked at or considered when you created an organizational structure?

Follow-on question 1: What was important?

Follow-on question 2: What was not important?

9. What, if anything, would you change about your decision on selecting a legal entity if you could?

Follow-on question 1: Why would you change this?

Follow-on question 2: Is there anything else about your decision on an organizational that you would like to elaborate on?

10. What other items should be added to our discussion?

10. Thank each subject for his or her participation in the study at the end of the interview.

11. Inform participants that a transcript of their interview will be made available to them when transcription is complete, and ensure participants understand they will have a final opportunity to clarify or add to responses.